# Design in general education

Eight projects
edited by John Harahan

Design Council

**Design in general education**
Eight projects

First edition published in the United Kingdom 1978 by
Design Council
28 Haymarket, London SW1Y 4SU

Designed by Gill Streater
Printed and bound in the United Kingdom by
Jolly & Barber Ltd, Rugby, Warwickshire
Distributed by
Heinemann Educational Books Ltd
48 Charles Street, London W1X 8AH

ISBN 0 435 86541 2 (paper)
ISBN 0 435 86540 4 (cased) ✔

© John Harahan 1978

# Contents

# Introduction

The reasons for the growth of design education in schools have already been well described in a number of publications, and recent investigations have been concerned more with attempts to understand the precise nature of the activity. It is in this area that I hope this book will make a contribution.

The things around us that are designed and made by man to a large extent determine the quality of our lives. We have sufficient knowledge and first-hand experience as a society to make great improvements in the way we live, provided that those responsible for making the decisions that affect all our lives operate within the framework of an informed and aware community, and are directly accountable to its members. Every effort should, I feel, be made to involve people in the planning and decision-making stages of projects that concern these material elements, whether they are, for example, manufactured goods, transport systems or housing. One way to improve general awareness is through education, and design education therefore commands a place in every school and for every child.

A few years ago, after a member of the 'Design in General Education' project team from the Royal College of Art visited an exhibition I had helped to organise about design work in the sixth form, my school was invited to set up a small display of work at the RCA the following year. I was then asked to join the project team as a research associate. The project was at that time funded up to the end of December 1975, and my school and education authority kindly allowed me to have unpaid leave of absence. I subsequently returned to teaching in January 1976.

I am starting from this point because it was during the eight months I spent working with the team at the Royal College of Art that I had the chance to travel extensively throughout the country, visiting schools and talking to teachers, and this allowed me to make a number of observations about the nature of design activity in schools. Some of these observations are, I feel, appropriate as an introduction to the accounts of projects that follow.

It became clear on talking to teachers that the term 'design education' was used in a variety of ways and that there was a considerable difference of opinion as to just what design education was all about. There were, however, a number of issues and areas of debate raised by teachers that did appear to emerge as having a common relevance. There were what could at best be called 'patterns' emerging that seemed to suggest ways of arriving at a better understanding of the many aspirations held by some schools and teachers. Without doubt, many teachers wanted to be involved with the development of design activity as a force to be reckoned with in schools, and this showed itself in widespread enthusiasm for its educational implications.

The reasons for the growth of design education are widely accepted. They include, for example, teachers' dissatisfaction with syllabus contents, the limited horizons of traditional subject boundaries, unrealistic learning programmes, the organisational developments arising from the growth of larger comprehensive units, and the injection of new courses precipitated by the raising of the school leaving age. But perhaps the most optimistic long-term aim of those concerned with design education in schools is a wish to involve students in what several teachers I spoke to called 'good educational experiences'. Although this is perhaps an obvious and general statement, the ways in which teachers try to achieve this objective are often complicated, and they are determined on a number of interacting levels.

Design education in schools can in one sense be described in terms of activities, and in this context it can be seen as involving a change of emphasis in the approach to learning that aims to clarify the individual student's response to his experiences, to map this progress and record its worth. Often this approach to learning uses a 'design brief' or 'project', and it is usually expected to take the student a fixed length of time. It follows that, if the time spent on such work is extensive, this must be taken into account in any assessment process. Often the only assessment made of a student's work is a close look at the 'end product'. The production of artefacts that are assumed to be worth-while ends in themselves, which can arise from attempts to transfer misunderstood, vestigial or derivative ideas from outside to serve as school models, is perhaps a questionable activity in schools. Merely looking at finished artefacts is not a sufficient way to measure the extent of learning, however great, that has taken place. One might argue further that this has clear implications for an examination system that is largely geared to assessing the 'end product', whether this is a formal test of memory and intellectual comprehension or some other artefact.

Terms such as 'problem solving' and 'open-ended problem solving' are often used to describe students' experiences in design education. In design research also, much time has been spent in examining designers' behaviour and methodology. But in an educational context, although the open-ended approach can be applied interestingly, one feels terms like these are often misunderstood. In particular there is, as one might perhaps expect, a great deal of variation in the extent to which teachers direct students towards certain kinds of understanding, and in the extent to which they leave students themselves to 'bridge the gap' between their initial understanding and a solution to a given problem. One example may help to illustrate the difficulties arising from such differing terminology.

In one school I visited, the woodwork department required 12-year-old boys to 'develop familiarity with certain joints, planing to size and working within limits'. The project began with the issue of a working drawing and a record sheet to each student ('In order to build up the routine and enable them to think systematically', said the teacher). The job was to produce a holder for a key or watch (described as 'something useful to be used on a bedside table, which may otherwise have to be purchased'). The open-ended aspects of the project were said to be that the design (which was no more than an excuse to joint two pieces of wood at a right angle) could be altered by varying the upright or horizontal dimensions. The teacher sincerely considered that he was allowing his pupils to develop through open-ended problem solving because they had a choice to make.

Of course, it would be unrealistic to generalise from this one example, but the whole question of the way in which open-ended problem solving is used as a technique for learning in schools needs to be thoroughly investigated if it is to be properly understood. Phil Roberts and I submitted a paper for the RCA Summer School in 1975, which aimed to raise questions about this aspect of design work in schools and, although it has been published elsewhere, I think it is worth recounting here:

Learning through activities that have been called 'designing', shares with the whole of the educational process the aim of promoting thought and personal growth by articulating possibilities for structuring experience.

If knowledge is in a state of continuous change how can we help children, and ourselves, develop attitudes, qualities, strengths, and insights appropriate to that condition?

An operational mechanism, for some, appears to lie in the development of 'problem solving' and we would like to focus on this, by asking a number of questions which we see as important and offering, in turn, some tentative answers for further discussion.

*What constitutes a problem?*

*What constitutes a solution?*

For discussion's sake, let us suppose that a typical activity might begin by the teacher asking the student, or agreeing with the student's wish to 'make a chair' (or, try another object).

*Is a chair a problem?*

*Or, is a chair a solution to a problem?*

*And if it is a solution, what then is the problem?*

*Or problems?*

*If it is a solution has the student considered other possible and valid responses?*

*And if 'yes' did he then redefine the problem? In other words, at what point did the student 'begin'?*

*Is a chair too particular, or can it throw light on the general?*

Apart from techniques of questioning, are there other mechanisms, for example in synectics and in brain-storming, to help students to arrive at some distinction between 'problems' and 'solutions' and to appreciate their interaction?

*If a chair is not a problem, how might we describe a problem?*

Some would suggest that a problem is a description of the process of sensing gaps or disturbing missing elements. In this sense, a 'solution' is an acceptable degree of closure of the gap. The gap, or incompatibility, or problem space, might be variously described as the difference between performance required and performance available; between aspirations and available skills; between preferred conditions and a present situation.

Problem solving is understood by some to consist in a sequential step-by-step process.

*For what kinds of problem might a step-by-step sequential 'design process' be sufficient?*

Might the student be enabled to see a chair as a product within a system (the home)? What is the relationship between product and system?

Does this suggest different kinds and levels of problem?

For instance, might it be helpful to consider the idea of the making of a chair as a technical problem?

Is it still possible for one procedure to be seen as appropriate to all problems?

Might a step-by-step procedure be most appropriate when there can be no possible deviation from a foreseen 'end'?

Is this kind of procedure algorithmic rather than heuristic?

Small scale and particular, rather than general?

Might there be differences in the structure of possible procedural approaches for, on the one hand, making *things* and on the other helping students expand their insights?

If there are differences, are they recognised both by adults and by students?

Can students be enabled to move towards some recognition that a 'methodology' is useful, but only sometimes sufficient?

Or is there a possibility that an attempt to provide a supportive structure for learning ('methodology') might be translated by an unacceptably large number of students and teachers as a closed prescription rather than as encouragement towards the opening of possibilities?

How can a 'method' (or '*the* method') be avoided and yet provide sufficient support for personal growth and change?

Or, might the question be one of enabling students to be at ease in a situation of risk? To enable them to undertake a practical consideration of the questions how? what? and why?

Can a situation which hopes to develop possibilities be evaluated?

What is to be evaluated; the experience, the product, or both?

And by whom?

*Can* problems be 'well defined'?

Might that mean 'only sufficiently'?

For instance, does the student's learning consist in simultaneously structuring as well as 'solving' a problem, with the problem space being continually modified?

*At what point, then, can a 'problem' be said to be solved or resolved, when*

*'its' context is a condition of change?*

It might be suggested that 'a problem' is a part of a continuing process, upon which part of our attention is presently focused.

*Do the opportunities in problem solving offer to the student the sense of being in a dynamic process, in the short term consisting of interlocking problems and also in the long term with changing environmental and individual contexts?*

If problem solving suggests a move away from the making of isolated products towards the consideration of products in their systematic context, what are the implications for the assumed parameters of subject boundaries?

In recent years there has been a fairly widespread use of professional design methodologies in schools as vehicles for learning. Often, equating design education with a 'logical approach' to work or curriculum structure seems to have given rise to misunderstanding and prejudice. It is perhaps not surprising when a wholesale transfer of, say, an engineering designer's methodology fails to provide a satisfactory learning experience in a school. Some might claim that such a transfer could help students to develop a more objective approach to their problems, but this may be of little relevance in the broad educational context.

Problem solving is often understood to consist of a series of sequential steps, but it would seem that these steps would be better termed patterns and, further, they do not appear to be automatic or mechanical. They are applied flexibly, according to the circumstances, and alternatives are available at every step. Much has been written about design methodology, but the solution of a problem in an educational context should, it seems to me, be primarily concerned with those aspects of the student's response to the problem that involve a search for decisions as to *how* to proceed. In other words, a student must be helped to develop his own methodology, in contrast to the frequent instances in which students and teachers see methodology as a closed prescription rather than an encouragement to look for further possibilities. Recent Schools Council projects in this field of design education have been criticised on these grounds.

A point that is crucial to the development of this attitude to design education appears to be that the student should understand the system within which he is working. On the one hand this might be thought of as the course structure or syllabus, but on the other it might be seen more fundamentally as involving the student's own understanding of his developing insights into his work. The 'doing' aspects of the system are the relevant processes, and these will have various starting levels. Both the teacher and the student must be aware of the level at which they enter a particular problem or learning situation.

Communication techniques also play an important part in design work in schools. I have already suggested that end products and artefacts can only be seen in relation to the overall experience and reasoning that lead to their development. It follows that communication of the working process and the student's relationship to the work are of fundamental concern if we are to examine and chart his progress. A more widespread acceptance of various methods of communication, including the use of tape recordings, photographs, notes and drawings, as well as writing, can allow students to develop their individual strengths. It is in this sense that design education can be thought of as *describing* the process of learning that a student has undertaken. Opening up opportunities to use all sorts of communication techniques can provide the basis for improved internal evaluation and justification as well as external validation.

Design as an activity relates thought and action in a very direct way, and evaluation of the process becomes continuous so far as the student is concerned. It is, I believe, essential to understand this if students are to be helped to develop a personal value in the work undertaken. Students can only develop such internal values, which underlie external evaluation, provided that work is 'realistic' to them.

Justification and verification ought not to be treated as separate procedures that occur only after the discovery of a solution to a problem. Rather, they should be included as part of the process of discovery itself. Proper communication of this process provides checkpoints for the external evaluator. Perhaps we can see opportunities here for encouraging students to assess themselves, although clearly it is one thing for students to evaluate the success or otherwise of their solutions, and quite another to assess the quality of their educational experiences.

Many teachers feel that design education activities naturally bridge whatever gaps have appeared between 'the two cultures' – aesthetics and science, or the qualitative and the quantitative. If one takes a simplistic model of a school orientated towards academic qualifications, one can see an argument for aesthetic experience to form an equal, if separate, part of the curriculum. The stronger the demands for paper qualifications and the louder the arguments about timetable allocations, the more weight is given to demands from teachers who want to develop students' qualitative experience. It is almost as if a vacuum is left in the middle, with each side becoming more and more polarised in an attempt to justify their position. A more realistic approach might be to try and combine qualitative and quantitative activities in some way, or at least to allow them equal development.

One can understand complaints from the defendants of the qualitative/intuitive camps when design activities are interpreted as being an attempt to reduce these aspects to procedural formulae. In particular, those devoted primarily to art education often express the fear that design education frequently makes use of a rigid, systematic design methodology, and while this can arguably be a help in the personal, educational and technical development of some students, it has obvious limitations for others. A better general understanding should allay these fears. The old belief that designing is a linear process that begins with a problem and ends with a solution must be even more radically modified by well-known concepts that show that the problem and solution formulations are inextricably mixed from the beginning of design procedures. Relating a 'logical' approach to the discovery of some kind of solution can provide a structure and a measure of creative tension. But a proper logic should reflect the continuous change and growth of real life, rather than imposing an unreal rigidity and precision.

Some teachers believe that design education can only operate within a confined range of subjects, but in fact the real implications of design education transcend subject areas and boundaries because the prime concern of design education is *developing approaches to learning*. In this light the development of design education can be seen to be central to the understanding that knowledge is part of the process of developing self-awareness by which individuals and societies reconstruct themselves.

As we know, knowledge is not static, and design education is evolving effective ways of enabling students to develop skills that prepare them to cope with change. Teachers change, students change, and learning reflects these changes. As teachers we should be concerned with providing the best possible conditions for encouraging positive attitudes to change. This is fundamental if tomorrow's citizens are to understand themselves in relation to each other and to their surroundings.

Some may argue that design education in schools is a belief

system and as such it can never become completely rational and consistent, since groups and individuals will always be resolving old conflicts and evolving new ones. Case studies can provide some useful information about the internal mechanisms and dynamics of the system. The case studies in this book are intended to give a glimpse of some aspects of what is a complicated picture. They are not intended to illustrate methods for repetition or for direct use as teaching aids – that would not do them justice. It is the narrowing of procedural options that makes teaching 'kits' inappropriate for developing relationships between particular personalities. I believe that to provide such kits is to miss the point and can only be a prescription for predictability.

The eight contributions that follow are from teachers who work in a variety of schools, and this has determined the order of presentation. Phil Roberts and Anne Constable both work in Middle Schools with pupils of 11 to 14, and John Jeffery and Nigel Billington describe work with boys of that age at Pocklington. Mike Stevenson teaches in a Grammar School for boys with students from 11 to 18. Phil Mason and Stephen Burroughs both work in Upper Schools with students from 14 to 18. Eileen Adams, Wilf Ball and myself have worked in Comprehensive Schools with students of 11 to 18.

All the contributors were asked to describe a particular project or piece of work that they considered showed design education in practice, with an emphasis on how the work was seen to develop by the student and the teacher, and using the students' own words wherever possible. As might be expected, all the contributors stress aspects they feel to be particularly important. Each case study is preceded by a short statement by the contributor that outlines the aims and objectives of the project, and is followed by brief details about the teachers themselves.

Phil Roberts uses his example to raise particular questions that can, however, be transferred to a more general context. Anne Constable outlines a second-year course concerned with design in the home based on a number of themes. John Jeffery and Nigel Billington give an account of some of the work of a basic design course they have developed concerned with conceiving, planning and making, while Mike Stevenson, Stephen Burroughs and myself describe some sixth-form work. Phil Mason shows how organising large groups of 15 and 16-year-olds can be made possible by using resources in the immediate school environment. Eileen Adams discusses aspects of her work on the Front Door project.

All the work described has social and environmental aspects. The case studies illustrate facets of design education in our schools today, but they can only provide a small sample of the enthusiasm, effort and determination of many teachers and students from many schools who have helped to make design education such an important part of a healthy, developing curriculum.

# Manor High School

## Phil Roberts

*Phil Roberts*

'*A number of aims and objectives appear to be pertinent to students working on graphic design problems in the design department at Manor High School. Apart from finding pleasure in creative activities, pupils are encouraged to develop their own creative ability to a high standard. A particular concern is that the pupil should understand the importance of visual media and forms of visual communication.*

'*Other definable areas arise from the work itself. Children may need to be helped to define situations and identify constraints and criteria; to propose acceptable responses; and to make decisions and evaluate their effects. Similarly, they may need assistance in the location and use of source material.*

'*Pupils ought to be encouraged to be aware of human needs and be flexible and adaptable in their work and in their attitudes towards others.*'

This piece of work, a piece of graphic design, is some evidence of a boy's design education experience. For present purposes I am not too interested in it as a product; my interest, rather, is in the fact that it provides some starting points for a consideration of the nature of the learning/designing process.

When this piece of work was done the boy was 13 years old, with only a slight interest in the institution of school, its affairs and values – or so it appeared, in terms of achievements. His one enthusiasm was in hand-setting type.

It is from there that we begin: an individual enthusiasm and an absence, as yet, of a real problem (that is to say, some experience of significance for the boy) upon which to focus and through which to develop his interest.

After a number of ideas had been floated and rejected by the boy, he thought some printing *for* someone might be worth working on. That was the germ of a 'design brief'. What was going on in the life of the school that might make use of print? Discussion and searching eventually pointed towards a festival of music and drama. What were the organisers doing about communicating with the likely or possible audiences? The answer appeared to be, 'Not very much', but to get even this far meant interviewing the staff and the pupils concerned with the festival, and formulating questions that would elicit the information required. He discovered there were two perspectives on this. First, what in fact was the information that the organisers required from their probable audiences and wished to transmit to their possible audiences; and, second, what was the information that he, the designer and printer, required in order to act on their behalf?

By this time, the boy was immersed in the project and moving fairly haphazardly towards planning his course of action. The point I want to make here is that he was not working to a 'brief'. His activity at this stage consisted of articulating the brief for himself. The brief, then, (which did not exist in the form of a statement at all) emerged from his questioning, and took a shape that enabled action to be taken. Indeed it was integral with action. He found that his questioning (almost incidentally and quite unexpectedly to him and perhaps to others) had the effect of sharpening the activities of the organisers of the festival, who were more concerned with the 'creative' side of the festival than with its (to them) less interesting administration. Until this rather idiosyncratic boy came along the precise details required, and being found, by him had been of peripheral importance. Here the point to be made is that the absence of a brief can in itself, on occasion, promote levels and kinds of activity that might otherwise be missed. Such a brief *could* have been formulated and given, however, perhaps something like this:

## Information to parents, and from parents to the school

Mr Hunt has sent out an explanatory letter of invitation to parents about the musical and dramatic activities of this term.

We need now to produce something (graphic) to act as a reminder (a fairly gentle one) and which will also provide us with some idea of the numbers coming.

Gather all the information from Mr Hunt and Mr Snelling (you will need to know, for instance, about how the tickets are going to be sold and distributed). Having gathered all the information, *you* are responsible for producing something

which will fulfil the requirements above. Some information:

1 Any colour of card can be ordered
2 Inks limited to colours in stock
3 Typefaces limited to those in stock
4 Finished job is required in two weeks
5 Keep all stages of the work
6 Work out all the costs

Such a brief would not have been unfamiliar or unreasonable (although this particular boy might not have found it very inviting had he been presented with it), but it would not have given the same opportunities for thinking for himself. In the event, *he* had to articulate the problem area, identify constraints and criteria of his possible valid responses and his eventual course of action.

In practice, even if a pupil does not start from a teacher-devised brief, it may well be necessary or useful for the pupil himself to be able to formulate one at some stage of his activity. Such a statement might be in written or oral form, or perhaps achieved through questioning. Apart from enabling the path ahead to be seen more clearly, it may also help as an evaluative, monitoring device or technique by showing the particular path that has been followed among the many possible paths. It may thus act as a review of the ways, the direction, and the manner and degree of change in the original situation that has happened in the learning/designing process. Such a review can answer the questions 'What alternative valid responses might you have made?' and 'Why are you doing this rather than . . .?' and thus illuminate the requirements to be fulfilled.

The process of changing is of course continuous and on-going, and there is, in this case, another important evaluative facet – the assessment of the impersonal product as a piece of graphic communication. To a large extent, the pupil could estimate the validity of his work from the return slips and refer back to earlier stages. For before committing himself in print it had been necessary for him to imagine the possible reaction of the people who received the note. Indeed, he had to occupy

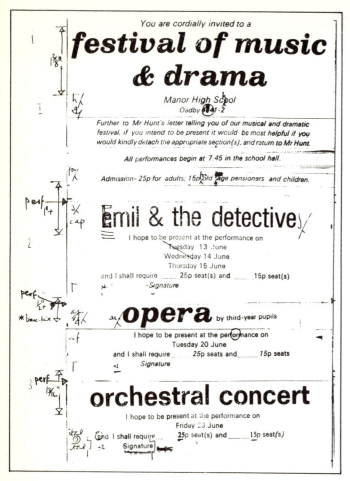

*The corrected proof.*

two positions, first as the maker of the message, and second, imagining himself as its recipient.

As an aside, the boy himself largely decided (or appropriated) the wording, the layout, founts, choice of materials, and organised a quite complicated sequence of steps. He found his most persistent constraint was time, rather than materials, facilities, or cost.

This particular episode produced a piece of graphic communication, and perhaps it raises a few questions.

Is there an underlying approach, or procedure, towards 'practical learning experience', a learning/designing process, that is generally appropriate irrespective of whether the end result might be two dimensional, three dimensional, or not in a material form at all?

How can we devise the institutional conditions that enable us to start from and focus on pupils' expressed interests and enable them not only to develop their enthusiasms but also serve subject requirements? This of course is to focus on the familiar problem of whether we are teaching children, or a subject, or children via the instrument of the subject.

How can we locate and use pupils' idiosyncratic interests to their educational advantage, and also avoid giving the perhaps familiar, though not entirely welcome, impression to colleagues that the art department is *merely* a convenient cheap printers?

How can we comprehend the more complex structure of work that is relatively heuristic compared with the more familiar 'algorithmic' kind of pre-set briefs? This necessarily means that the teacher, by virtue of his greater experience, must recognise and accept the responsibility for possible 'failure' (real failure perhaps in the mind of the pupil) that is implicit in heuristic activity of the kind described in this article. How can we ensure a balance for the pupil of route-following activity towards public knowledge and route-finding towards personal knowledge?

*Phil Roberts is Head of Design and Curriculum Adviser at Manor High School, Oadby, Leicestershire. The school is an 11–14 mixed comprehensive, and the Design Department is open plan and purpose built. Students work from briefs that become progressively more demanding in terms of skill and intellect. The organisation is fairly fluid and allows opportunity for integrated work to develop naturally.*

*Phil Roberts was General Secretary for the National Association for Design Education for six years.*

festival of music
& drama

You are cordially invited to a

Manor High School
Oadby 4941-2

... Hunt's letter telling you of our musical and ...
... ou intend to be present it would be m... ...
... ly detach the appropriate section(s), an...

All performances begin at 7.45 in the ...

...ission- 25p for adults: 15p for old age ...

**orchestral concert**

I hope to be present at the performance on
Friday 23 June
and I shall require ___ 2 ___ 25p seats and ___ 15p seats
Signature  *Geoffrey White*

**Emil & the detectives**

I hope to be present at the performance on
Tuesday 13 June
Wednesday 14 June
Thursday 15 June
___ 25p seats and ___ 15p seats
Signature

**Emil & the detectives**

I hope to be present at the performance on
Tuesday 13 June
Wednesday 14 June
Thursday 15 June
... require  3 ... 25p seats and ___ 15p seats
...  *F. Smith*

**an opera** by third-year pupils

I hope to be present at the performance on
Tuesday 20 June
and I shall require  2  25p seats and  10  15p seats
Signature  *Peter Brown*

**an opera** by third-year pupils

I hope to be present at the performance on
Tuesday 20 June
___ 25p seats and ___ 15p ...
and I shall require ___ 25p seats and ___ 15p seats
Signature

**orchestral concert**

I hope to be present at the performance on
Friday 23 June
and I shall require  0  25p seats and  4  15p seats
Signature  *Rosemary Green*

**orchestral conce...**

I hope to be present at the performance on
Friday 23 June
___ 25p seats and ___ 15p seats
and I shall require ___ 25p seats and ___ 15p seats
Signature

# Stonehill High School

## Anne Constable

*Anne Constable*

*'How does design in the home differ from Home Economics? Basically there is a shift of emphasis from the specific topics of previous years to wider design themes. This does not mean, as many people often feel, that we 'dabble' in this and that! It does mean that we approach a topic from a wider viewpoint, and that we introduce skills and basic methods, but instead of being isolated we relate them to other work so that they become more meaningful to the child. We still encourage the satisfaction of creating with food, as well as trying to cater for our jet-age eating habits. With the ever-increasing weight of criticism being levelled against our over-processed foods, we try to encourage students to look critically at their eating habits and to investigate the properties of food-stuffs, thereby giving them greater understanding of the materials from which we build our bodies.*

*'Food, family and home are vitally important in our present-day, mass-produced, mass-media society. It is only by independent thought and work that we can hope to influence our lives. Design gives us the freedom to discover, and the opportunity to release the individuality within each of us.'*

Before the new school year in 1975 we decided that it was time to review our second-year design course. After much discussion, we produced a scheme whereby a group of 22 students became attached to a design tutor for one term. Within this structure, student mobility was encouraged as and when work necessitated it.

The four elements – earth, air, fire and water – were to be our starting points, one element being the theme for each term. Every student in the department was given a design brief on the current theme from which to develop scrapbooks and practical pieces of work.

All members of staff introduced the theme as they wished, with emphasis on their own specialisation. Within the two home economics rooms we always had two different courses running simultaneously, one biased towards food, the other towards the home, although for the beginning of each course we often considered the same type of work.

Staff looked at the widest aspects of the topic, and we tried to obtain appropriate project information from the library. After looking at and discussing films, slides and pictures, each student recorded several illustrated definitions about one element – which, in the following example, was air. Generally the final points were decided by the class as a whole and led into the appropriate work for the course, being concerned either with food or the home.

Certain relevant teaching points were felt necessary in the light of discussions with the students:

Early man lived purely on the fruit, vegetables and nuts that he could find around him. Later he began hunting, and added meat and animal produce, such as eggs to his diet.

Then he learnt how to cultivate crops and so cereals became important.

As we became more civilised, so did our food, and we ate more floury and sugary foods and less of the simple fruit, vegetables and meat.

Today if we look at our menu, it is widely different from our ancestors'.

We eat many made-up foods and our meals are very different from those eaten by our predecessors.

As yet no generation of people has become old, having lived on today's foods with their cumulative total of food additives inside their bodies.

We have too much food to choose from so we must try and choose wisely.

We should try and choose something from man's early diet. These foods are important for protecting our bodies against diseases – fresh fruit, nuts and vegetables. We should also include milk, cheese, cocoa, liver and fatty fish.

Then we should choose something from the hunting diet – meat, fish, animal products, milk, cheese, eggs – or use peas, beans, nuts, lentils or soya products. These foods are important for growth and repair of the body. We should fill up with the cereal and sugary foods. These, with fats like butter and lard, give us extra energy.

Then, by means of posters, displays and discussion, these

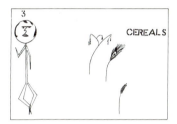

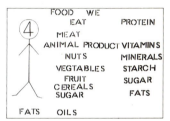

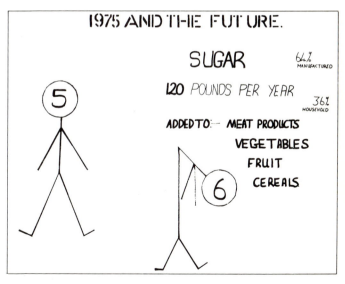

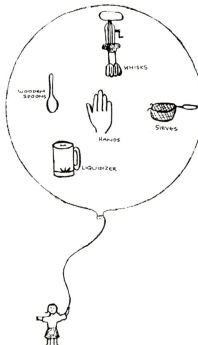

points were used as a means of introducing basic nutrition. Thus, when practical cookery began the students were encouraged to evaluate all recipes, and see them as part of the day's meals, or more importantly as a spectrum of the foods they feed into their bodies. The question was raised 'What is the result?', and this led on to an understanding of how we influence our health by the food we eat.

'We eat food to keep us alive, and we should try to eat a selection of foods at each meal so that our bodies may grow and repair any damage, protect us from disease, and give us energy to live.'

Consideration was also given to the fact that air expands on heating and reference was made to the pupils' work in the science department and experiments they had done.

Two experiments were demonstrated in class. A tin with the lid pressed on was boiled in a pan of water until the lid flew off, and a balloon was blown up, then placed in the drying cabinet. This burst when the air expanded from the heat. Thus we began to see the effect of air expansion, so that we knew that when air was introduced into food and the food was heated it would expand even further, and mixtures like batters, soufflés, meringues, sponges and pastry would become light.

We also considered how air could be introduced into mixtures by mechanical means, and lessons then followed where the class investigated the fact that certain foods can 'hold' air bubbles. We used the fact that some liquids can hold air to make sponges, meringues and milk shakes.

Each student made a milk shake as a simple introduction to the room and routine organisation. After this introduction the practical lessons were devoted to looking more fully at the ways air could be incorporated into mixtures by sieving, rubbing, creaming and whisking. Each student was expected to keep a record of the practical work, preferably illustrated. Also the food value of the recipe had to be included.

After this initial period there could be a change over of students. Some left the group to work in other areas. For example, one boy decided that the size and shape of the wooden spoon he had used for creaming was unsatisfactory for the shape of the bowl he used, so he visited the woodwork area to experiment with the shapes of spoons. Another boy had been investigating air and the weather as part of his booklet and at this point he decided he would like to make a weather-vane.

Other students arrived to join the group, either to pursue a set idea of their own or to join in a class project. In order to give the new students a satisfactory starting point, and to give the original students a chance to recap on their experience, they made a 'clear stage recipe' such as a lemon meringue pie, thus introducing or recapping on air in mixtures by sieving and rubbing in, as well as progressing to some degree by using egg whites. Again, we referred back to the experiments and noted how the addition of sugar stabilises the froth and forms a meringue.

The following week we looked at the introduction of air into pastry by rolling and folding. For practical work flaky pastry was made into sausage rolls and pies.

In order to try and look at as many links as possible with air and food, one session was spent looking at the range of cooking fats available that have air already whipped into them. We then used several of these fats to make a pastry recipe again, but this time using the method recommended by the various manufacturers.

At this stage the majority of the group had become familiar with the basic principles involved in the organisation of work with food. They now had four weeks in which students could develop the work as they felt appropriate. With co-operation and discussion at home and school, each student planned out the weeks' work. They had to give reasons for their choice of foods, and hand in the four-week time plan, together with the recipes, during the previous week. This enabled recipes to be checked for faults, difficult aspects that needed help to be emphasised and gave time for further discussion with their families if there were any alterations.

Some students continued with new recipes while others, using the previous methods, progressed to more complex recipes. One or two students decided to investigate entirely new work, for example the effect of different gases, using raising agents such as yeast. Others decided to attempt to use animal and plant foods more specifically.

Concurrent with this work each student was asked to investigate the equipment used for putting air into food. Finding out about as many pieces of equipment as possible, drawing them and finding pictures, costing them, listing their advantages and disadvantages, and judging 'value for money' were all aspects of their investigations. Special reference was made to any modifications of equipment that had taken place over the years, and the reasons for them were noted.

At the end of the weeks' individual work we made several joint conclusions about food and air. Each student then summarised his or her own term's work, showing dishes prepared, their accompaniments and a suitable menu, checking that they had made a varied choice of menus by including a generalised nutrient list.

Thus at the end of the term each student had some feeling for creating with food. They had some understanding about the foods available and the importance of being able to see that all the food eaten during one day had longer-term effects. They were able to build up a general picture of the food they ate in a year, so that they came to realise for themselves that over a long period of time their bodies may be short of certain nutrients and disease may develop from deficiencies. I was particularly concerned with this aspect of the students' experience because it is terribly hard to change our eating habits and it is really only by increased awareness and enthusiasm for food that we can make some positive change to our eating patterns. Thus, capturing some of the enthusiasm of the students by involving them individually with their own families' meals, we were able to introduce one or two ideas into their home menus.

The theme of air was also developed in the sessions devoted to housecraft. Some of the final points were listed by the students as being significant:

Air is the gaseous substance surrounding the earth.

Air is made up of a mixture of gases – oxygen, hydrogen, nitrogen and carbon dioxide.

Country air has usually 0.03 per cent $CO_2$; in the cities there is usually a higher proportion of $CO_2$ because of the pollution from industry and transport.

Most of the air contains some moisture; even on a hot summer day it will contain some water vapour.

The work by the group considered how they were personally affected:

'Air is the space around us – our surroundings, and it affects us in our homes.'

It was noted that early man had a very simple dwelling compared with our present day homes. His home had to provide shelter, protection from weather and animals and provide somewhere to eat and sleep. Since his daily life was restricted to the essentials of living, one room was sufficient.

It was generally concluded that because our lives are so complex we need several rooms inside our dwelling so that we have sufficient space for all our jobs and hobbies. At this point the students looked more closely at the history of dwellings, up to the present day.

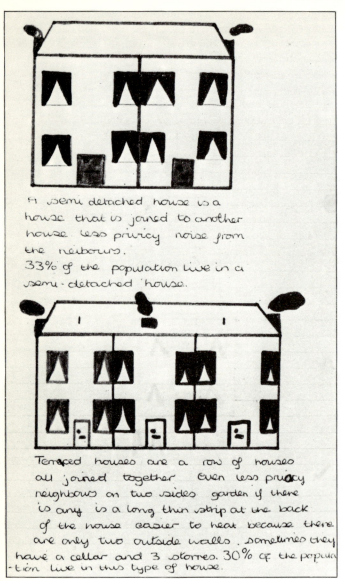

A semi detached house is a house that is joined to another house less privicy noise from the neibours.
33% of the population live in a semi-detached house.

Terraced houses are a row of houses all joined together even less privacy neighbours on two sides garden if there is any is a long thin strip at the back of the house easier to heat because there are only two outside walls. sometimes they have a cellar and 3 storries. 30% of the popula-tion live in this type of house.

A walk into the village provided the basis for further discussion on the different types of dwellings. Each student made sketches of detached and semi-detached houses, terraced houses, bungalows, flats and maisonettes. In class, further

discussion of the advantages and disadvantages of each type of dwelling took place.

Using local newspapers, each student collected advertisements of all the different types of dwellings. Drawing a very simple map of the town showing the major roads only, the advertisements were placed in the approximate areas. This

promoted discussion about house prices and the influence of certain areas and amenities on their value.

The project was then brought back to a more individual stand, each student being asked to draw in simple form the space needed by his or her family.

This piece of work then developed in many ways, one student considered the space available in any room, and investigated how it could best be utilised and furnished. A group of students, however, chose to investigate storage in the kitchen.

To lead into considering kitchen planning (using the space available in the kitchen to the best advantage), the group made a simple Victoria sandwich recipe. The aim here was to choose a recipe using staple ingredients that most people would have in stock. At the same time it was a straightforward recipe for introducing the group to room organisation and routine for working with food.

The students made a careful record of the equipment used, methods of preparing and cooking, clearing away and presentation of the finished dish. From these notes they drew a flow diagram showing the path they would take in their own kitchens to make the recipe.

The class as a whole looked at the flow diagrams and they inspired quite a lot of discussion about kitchen layouts. It also provided the opportunity for several students, who were particularly interested in this aspect of the work, to move to another area of design and re-style their own kitchen by careful planning and model making. After considering the various

shapes of kitchen layouts, the group turned to look more specifically at storage space in the kitchen.

Discussion took place as to what the most important pieces of kitchen equipment were, then each student became responsible for particular pieces of equipment. Each article was drawn on a master sheet, so that the pupils were able to duplicate off a leaflet entitled *Essential Equipment for a Kitchen*. Still using the same articles, the students were asked to comment on the storage and care of their particular piece of

equipment, with particular emphasis on any design modifications which could improve the article, such as 'stackability'.

Returning to food, the group looked at the dry ingredients each family generally kept in stock. Comments about the correct storage of these foods led into another food lesson, the activity of which might have developed from the brief: 'Using all dry ingredients except for two, choose a suitable recipe'.

This tended to be self limiting, but at this stage it was important that the students did not embark on too many varied ideas. However, it introduced to the group the prospect of finding their own recipe with consultation at home. Any student who had difficulty with choosing a recipe was given more specific guidance. It was decided that ready-prepared dried foods were worthy of closer inspection, so each individual chose one packet mix to bring along and prepare.

The students found that the packets themselves were particularly interesting, some were very attractive, taking up a lot of storage space yet containing a small volume of ingredients.

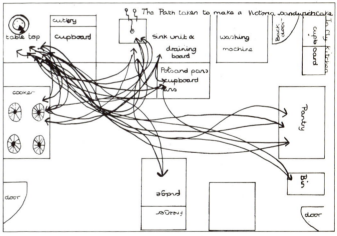

The list of ingredients in each packet promoted another discussion lesson. The additives provided another link with science, since the pupils were able to look at some of these chemicals in their raw, physical state. Information gathering and discussion about dry ingredients ended with a tape recording about instant coffee, and was rounded off by a 'coffee tasting' session, the students considering the 'best value for money'.

Tinned foods were the group's next consideration. A display of the various foods available in tins, and comments about the advantages and disadvantages of storing and using tinned foods started off the topic.

The students listed the tinned foods used by their family and what they were used for. Practical cookery involved one of their own family's recipes that used any tinned food. All the tins and labels were saved and this naturally led into the next lesson. Once again we discussed packaging, particularly the sizes of tins and labels, and the ease of opening. Ideas about restyling can sizes and altering labels were talked about and each student designed a label that showed what he or she considered to be important information.

The group then turned to cleaning materials. A collection of all the different types of cleaning materials commonly used in the home was grouped together with any appropriate equipment. After class discussion, groups of students investigated certain cleaning stuffs in more detail – metal polishes, washing-up liquids, washing powders, furniture polishes, bath and sink cleaners. Each group presented their findings by a small display, poster or collage and gave a short talk to the rest of the class.

The topic was concluded by discussing the storage of cleaning materials with regard to their safety and potential danger in the home.

The group returned to food storage and particularly to considering fresh foods. Firstly fruits and vegetables that may be kept in a fruit bowl or vegetable rack were listed and notes were made of the importance of freshness for maximum food values, and how produce deteriorates, and food value is reduced as storage time increases. To make this work more realistic the group tested some fruits and vegetables which had been stored for specific times for their vitamin C content. The results were recorded on a colourful chart, which the students designed. Their idea was to make an impressive poster that would publicise better storage of these foods.

Secondly, the group considered other fresh foods that were normally kept in the refrigerator – meat, eggs, milk and fats. All the families in this particular group owned a refrigerator, so for homework the students drew their own particular model, marking in the foods they kept in it. Along with this they included a list stating the uses of the various foods. At this stage the practical cookery was a class recipe, thus allowing any new members of the group to become familiar with the methods of working with food. Either quiches Lorraines or egg custards were made, using fats, milk and eggs stored in the refrigerator and a group discussion of storage times for foods

and refrigerator hygiene concluded this aspect of housecraft.

From the refrigerator, the group looked at home freezers, comparing the two different types, both chest and upright. Once again parental co-operation was encouraged by asking for suggestions for practical work which could be put in a freezer. As an alternative, pupils were able to stock up the school freezer. Work naturally developed and in the class we investigated batch baking, blanching vegetables, tray freezing fruits, freezing raw pastry – choux puffs – and freezing liquids – soup and sauce. Correct storage times were emphasised and the importance of packaging and correct temperatures. Some students in the group used commercial frozen food, noting its impact on our food habits.

A discussion and display around the school freezer enabled everyone to make a visual record of foods stored in this way. A film on frozen food shown to the group recapped on the essential information.

To conclude this storage topic each member of the group was asked to design and make a model of some form of storage unit that would be useful in a kitchen. Although many old ideas were used, several new inventions were produced, including a knife sharpener and storage unit that could be set into the wall so that knives always came out ready sharpened.

On reflection the students seemed to enjoy this work; the information gathered from their own kitchens usually meant that there had been some discussion of the project at home. All students, whatever their ability, had some visual record of the work which could serve as a guide or reminder about kitchen planning for their future home. Most important was the enthusiasm and understanding generated within the group for the project. Each individual had been able to experience and complete something worthwhile, whether through drawings, charts, tape recordings, models, leaflets, or practical cookery. At the end of every term each student completes an assessment sheet. This records the work undertaken during the course, marks gained and any relevant comments by the student and members of staff.

In order to give some idea of how the students' experiences are developed throughout the Design Department as a whole, I would like to finish with an account from a project booklet.

'A third of the earth's surface is covered by land, and the land is partly covered by homes. So we decided to do a topic on homes. We collected together pictures of houses and drew pictures of our home; the different rooms etc. Then we learnt

## 2nd YEAR DESIGN · MOVEMENT & MARK SHEET

NAME Julie Oldham          FORM 2LS          GROUP 3B band

TUTOR Mrs. Constable          THEME Earth          AREA Home E

WORK DONE SO FAR
cookery
We have investigated the diet of man from pritaras
carnivorous, herbivorous, omnivores up to this day

ASSESSMENT

FIRST CHANGE (Subject & Teacher) Pattern and Print
                                  Mrs Morris
WORK INTENDED
kitchen decoration - Printed Wall Hanging.

CHANGE APPROVED                    .Sig H.H. Date

ASSESSMENT  Screen Print of Fruit  (A)

SECOND CHANGE (Subject & Teacher) WOODWORK MR LOFTHOUSE

WORK INTENDED  a fruit bowl

CHANGE APPROVED                   A Sig          Date .

ASSESSMENT Good Imaginative Ideas. Wooden Fruit Bowl (A)

THIRD CHANGE (Subject & Teacher)

WORK INTENDED

CHANGE APPROVED                    Sig          Date

ASSESSMENT

END OF COURSE ASSESSMENT AND SUMMARY (including Theme Booklet)

B+ / A   A very varied course, including Food,
         Printing and Woodwork. Julie planned
         all the work herself and followed through
         the ideas with good practical results.

B+       Booklet, well presented & organised.

                                  Sig A.E.C. Date

---

where we looked into the water content of foods and its importance to the body.

'For my third year, I hope to use "the home" as my theme. I would like to make a coffee table, floor cushion, hostess apron, a set of mugs and do some cake and biscuit cookery. I enjoy having the opportunity to plan my own work and giving "something of me" to the end product.'

*Anne Constable is Head of the Home Economics Department at Stonehill High School, Leicestershire, an 11–14 mixed comprehensive. In the Creative Design Department students in the first year rotate through all the major areas of the department, following a new theme each time. Every theme is introduced by films, slides etc, and ends with an exhibition of the work from the whole department. Students also have a theme booklet. In the second year the pattern of the first year is continued. Each term a new theme is presented and a different area of design investigated. After an initial period in their set areas students may move anywhere in the department as their project dictates, or according to their natural interest. Thus they begin to develop their own personal design course within the framework of the current theme. This continues as a four unit course into the first term of the third year. In the third year the emphasis is on the individual. Each student reviews his experience in design over the last two years and builds from this his own personal design course. Thus the student has a chance to explore and experiment with media of his own choice and to achieve a detailed personal study of his own.*

---

how to do the practical jobs connected with a home.
Air had to be interpreted in light and colour. We drew using pencil crayons, pictures and plans of our environment. I made a model of a stained glass window.

'Using the hot flames we bent metal and I turned mine into a stainless steel bangle. This was rather a basic interpretation of the "Fire" theme. In cookery we investigated the effect of heat on foodstuffs. The "Water" theme I began in the Art Room. Using clay, inks, pencils, paint and felt tip pens we did several designs incorporating ideas about water. Then on to cookery,

# Pocklington School
## Nigel Billington and John Jeffery

*Nigel Billington*

*John Jeffery*

*'We believe that the teaching of design in secondary schools is best achieved through an integrated approach rather than separate art, craft and technology courses. We have developed a basic course that aims to give a strong impulse to creative design through a disciplined and ordered series of experiences, but which is at the same time 'geared' to the age and experience of the children. In the first three years we believe that the approach to all design problems needs to be biased towards intuitive responses and reasoning. Beyond this age, which approximates to the beginning of adolescence, we feel that a fresh approach is needed that:*

*1 leads towards a conscious and critical awareness of ethical, emotional and aesthetic values, technical possibilities and the ability to make valid intellectual decisions (Design Awareness)*

*2 extends and improves the facility to bring ideas to physical fruition (Design Activity)*

*3 makes conscious the experience and satisfaction of creative activity that will, one hopes, last into adult life.*

*Our concern at Pocklington School is primarily with activity. In this, we include the complete spectrum, from the arousal of curiosity in the natural and man-made worlds, through the process of data gathering, speculation and planning to the physical "wroughting" involved in the making of artefacts.'*

The Design Centre at Pocklington School opened in January 1970, bringing together under one roof an existing Art Department and a new Technical Unit. From the outset it was decided that the Centre should develop an integrated approach to the teaching of art, craft and technology so that, from starting in the school at the age of 11+, all boys would have the intellectual stimulation and creative satisfaction of 'conceiving and making' in ways appropriate to their age. The activity of conceiving, planning and making things has always been one of the most vital forces in the life of a civilised people. This broad area of human endeavour is 'design' and has resulted in artifacts as diverse as the Mona Lisa, a pin and a laser. Modelling is the language of design. How an object is to be shaped, its proportions and organisation, how its parts fit together and the mechanism by which it might operate are all principally communicated through drawings, plans and models. However, in order to conceive, plan and make successfully, it is necessary to understand and experience how it has been done before – one must be aware of design before one can actively design.

The teaching of design (including engineering) in schools, especially to the younger child, must, we believe, be through a carefully structured and widely based course that enables the child to become fluent in drawing and modelling techniques and capable of responding imaginatively to demands on his ingenuity, aesthetic and emotional sensibility and craft skills. Thus the course must pay specific attention to three vital elements:

1 The arousal of curiosity in the natural and man-made worlds through the processes of observation and analysis, which give an awareness of form and other aesthetic values and a knowledge of prior art.
2 The opportunity for speculative thought and the exercise of ingenuity.
3 The development of the facility to bring ideas to physical fruition.

The first element is concerned with the development of design awareness and is essential to fuel the imagination. This design awareness, and a fluency in the language of modelling, is achieved by a study of how things look, feel, work and behave. The young designer develops his experience of the structural, technical and aesthetic qualities in the world around him by an analysis of natural forms, physical processes and man-made objects, and increases his ability to communicate these experiences through drawing, modelling and handling materials. It is only through a study of the natural world that he will gain a feeling for the quality of organic vitality, growth and change that is so vital to a fully developed sense of design awareness and without which man divorces himself from nature.

Secondly, the ability to speculate – to think divergently – is at the root of creativity. It is the enjoyment of living with uncertainty, of holding the threads of different ideas in unresolved suspension, of drawing inspiration from unlikely sources and of speculating that characterises the designer. Also, when the occasion demands it, he must be able simultaneously to juggle technical ideas with aesthetic sensibility and constructional details with emotional responses, blending, rationalising and distilling them by means of models and drawings into a new entity. This leap into design activity is virtually impossible without the 'data gathering' input of design awareness.

Without the last of the three elements – a facility with craft skills – no worthwhile product can result. Clearly though, the conceptual stages precede 'making' and no amount of emphasis on craft skill can compensate for a lack of design preparation. A completely successful artefact must have been well conceived and developed as an idea, but it must also be made to the highest standard possible.

Although the processes of investigation, speculation and fabrication have been referred to separately, they are all important and are present at each stage in the design process. For example, the investigatory and analytical activity that develops the awareness of design is carried out through exercises in drawing and modelling, but speculation and imaginative thought inevitably take place at the same time. Likewise the school workshop is as much for learning and experiment as it is a production unit, and a further flow of creativity and spontaneous change can take place at this stage as the child becomes more aware of the properties of materials and the use of tools.

We shall illustrate this approach, and the way in which the course functions, by describing one of the themes that is central to the whole course and provides the hinge pin of much of the work in the second year.

The aspect of design that we wish to pay specific attention to is that of proportion, structure and the interplay of parts. A quick examination of anything will show that it can be thought of as being made up of a number of parts. In the design of an artefact, be it a painting, a chair or a bicycle, it is the proportioning of the parts in themselves and one to another that is the prime consideration. Shape, form, weight, mass, function and balance must all be considered if an elegant and coherent whole is to be achieved. Structure is very closely related to proportion; in fact the two quickly become inseparable as the problem of how parts are to fit, interlock, turn and move together is considered.

For example, a picture is essentially a two-dimensional organisation of shapes (maybe representing three-dimensional forms) and it is primarily the proportions of each shape in itself and the relationships between the shapes that produces a sense of structure and the necessary sense of overall harmony and coherence. Equally, a good bicycle will be well proportioned in its parts, but here their mechanical and structural function will have influenced their size and shape and hence the overall proportions of the machine.

These aspects of proportion and structure are central to all designing, and thus they figure prominently throughout the course. We shall illustrate the way in which we develop these concepts by choosing examples from work done in the 12+ to 13+ age range, and will also show, through these illustrations, how technical concepts, drawing and craft skills, and aesthetic and emotional responses are simultaneously developed.

The second year begins with a discussion of what the eye sees in natural forms and man-made objects. Through a process of question and answer, we come to realise that man makes objects because of need; he sees a problem and solves it by designing and making something. We see that this is how man is able to clothe and feed himself; how he builds homes, factories, roads, railways; how he brings about the environment in which he and his children will live.

Continuing the discussion, ideas concerning the present and a more ideal world emerged:

'All families should live in small but well designed houses.'

'Towns and cities should not be too big.'

'There are too many things, the essential ones should last longer and be more efficient.'

'People should get together more to plan the kind of places they would like to live in.'

'Beautiful and well designed things help people to be happier.'

How might we achieve a better place to live in?

'By people looking at the mess that is around them and seeing what is wrong with it.'

'By looking at well designed things and finding out what is good about them.'

'By looking how nature does it.'

These and a number of other comments finally led to the following conclusions:

1 That it is very important to look at things and assess their value and efficiency.

2 That it is important to study and absorb the proportion, shape, form, pattern, structure and mechanics of good and beautiful things, and that this is best done by drawing or modelling them. For it is by observing and analysing things that one comes to understand them, and having done this one is in a much better position to conceive, plan and make efficient and beautiful things oneself.

3 Finally, that natural forms might be better than man-made things for first study, since no matter how hard he tries, man cannot escape nature.

At this point the children were given something specific to study (this year it was green peppers), which they cut open and examined. As a direct result of the earlier discussion the children quickly realised that it was important to have a clear understanding of what they were looking for, and how they might set about recording it. It is interesting to note that many of the class could contribute a fair amount of biological information, which helped in identifying the structure and nature of the material's substance.

However, it was appreciated that the pepper had other qualities – a tough outer skin and soft inner walls, an interior divided into cavernous compartments, and bunched seeds. It was also established that it was the proportion and structure of the parts in themselves, and in relation to one another, that created the elegance of the assembly and the beautiful completeness of the whole. As the discussion progressed comments were made such as:

'Natural forms seem to be made up of a number of parts and so when you draw them you will get a repetition of similar shapes and patterns.'

At this point it was possible to concentrate the children's attention towards either the three-dimensional 'containing quality' of the form, or the essentially two-dimensional pattern of the parts revealed in cutting open the pepper. Parallels were drawn between these qualities as revealed in the pepper and the same qualities in artefacts and other natural forms.

The children then proceeded to produce several drawings of the pepper in which they explored both its three-dimensional containing aspect and its two-dimensional decorative and pattern qualities, in the knowledge that their work was not only an exercise in drawing skill, but had value as a starting point for their future two and three-dimensional work.

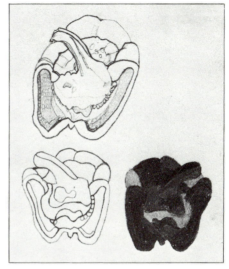

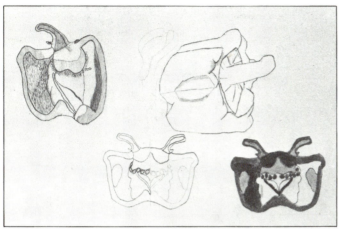

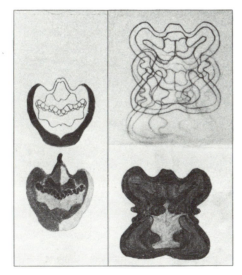

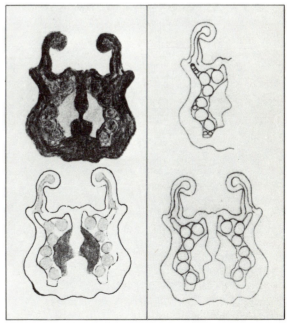

We have described this data-gathering activity first as we believe it to be the prerequisite of all design activity. The basic pattern of the boys' experiences during this second year is

summarised in the diagram, but it only serves as a framework and we are always ready to modify it in the light of our experience, or that of the children.

Everyone with experience of a school workshop will readily call to mind the well-intentioned 12-year-old who has the utmost difficulty in presenting an idea on paper – or otherwise – and whose idea of a workshop drawing conveys woefully little information.

'Please sir, can I make *this*?'

There follows a protracted question, answer and suggestion session to complete and clarify the idea to the point at which he can actually start to do something.

This sort of drawing skill is quite different from the usual observational and analytical drawing in which the 'object' is already there to be seen. For when something new is being conceived it starts its life as a mental picture in the mind of the designer and it is vital that he is able to explore and record a rapid succession of images as his ideas develop. We call this skill 'conceptual drawing' or sketch designing, and we give it equal attention in the course to the data-gathering process of analytical and observational drawing.

We introduce the children to this technique in the second year of the course (12+) because this is the age at which they have acquired some basic craft skill and are beginning to want to use the workshop in their own time for making things, from bookshelves to rabbit hutches.

Thus we deliberately set out, through a structural series of exercises, to develop this ability first to conceive and then to represent on paper a mental idea consisting of several three-dimensional forms interlocking and penetrating one another.

## Pattern of work in the second year of the design course at Pocklington School

**1 Looking at the natural world and looking at man-made objects**
Observational and analytical drawing of fruits, flowers, plants and simple mechanical objects.

**2 Development of conceptual drawing skills and mechanical ideas**
Directed drawing of simple geometric forms; oblique and perspective sketching.
Observation and analysis of mechanisms. Conceiving of interlocking, interpenetrating and moving geometric forms.
Rationalisation in terms of available material, and basic method of orthographic projection.
Sketch designing leading to workshop fabrication.

**3 People**
Discussion of the mechanical structure of the body, basic movements and postures, proportion, and contraposto.
Freer and more emotional experiments with wrestling, marching and intertwining figures.
Graphic expression of changing positions, choices and situations.
Clay modelling of dramatic groups.

**4 Decorative craft work in wire, etching and cloisonné techniques**
Stylised development of the observational and analytical drawings done in (1).
Sensitivity and work on a jewellery scale.
Variety of craft techniques.

The first stage is to give a session over to the teaching of quick, freehand sketching of simple geometrical forms, with an emphasis on developing a sense of parallelism, squareness and quality of line. After introducing either a basic isometric or oblique sketching technique, the children are asked to draw an

imagined cube; to 'stretch' it into a rectangular block, to 'flatten' it into a slab; and then to consider the block being pierced by simple holes and slots.

Parallel to this, as a mental fantasy, the boys were asked – what is a citadel?

'A city on a hill.'

'A fortified city.'

'A compact and well organised city with clear boundaries.'

They were asked to imagine this in their mind's eye and to build it on the table with wooden blocks. The children then drew part of this 'architectural' arrangement using coloured pencils and paying particular attention to colour, tone, proportion and positioning. In this situation the problem becomes that of portraying the mass of the blocks and the volume of the spaces between them – an interplay of volumes of solid and volumes of space.

The development of conceptual drawing skill was taken a step further in a way that extended the first of these exercises to include simple mechanical ideas. The children were shown photographic slides of earth-moving machinery – couplings, pistons, valves and other parts of railway engines – and actual mechanisms such as a car differential and a motor cycle gear-

box. In all cases the emphasis was on boldly mechanical devices dramatically presented, and although slides are once removed from the real thing, they can more than compensate for this in visual power. The boys responded readily in the subsequent discussion and could appreciate the variety of ways in which the sliding, rubbing, turning, pivoting, inter-slotting and interlocking of parts had been arranged.

Stimulated by the excitement of these mechanical actions, the boys were then asked to imagine an arrangement of blocks that consisted of, for example, a number of interlocking parts which, by virtue of their shape, could be put together in a variety of ways, or perhaps could be interslotted, turned or moved on one another. This exercise linked back to the fantasy of the citadel exercise in that the boys were concerned with the same variability of association plus, now, the possibility of an intriguing uncertainty of position and the demand on their conceptual powers was extended from the static to the dynamic situation.

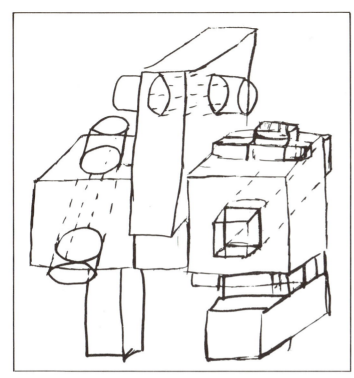

Quite often a boy used actual blocks to help him visualise a particular arrangement, but a final mental visualisation was imposed on him in the act of sketching his arrangement since a complete mock-up was just not possible with solid blocks. Once a satisfactory idea had formed it was then a matter of exploring the effect of altering the proportion of parts (through

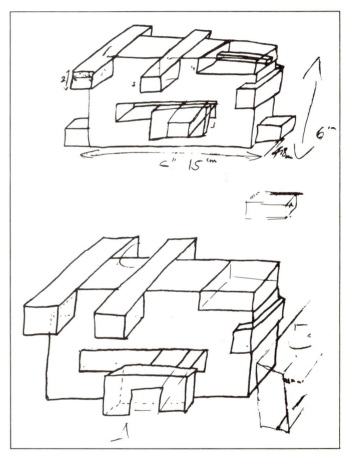

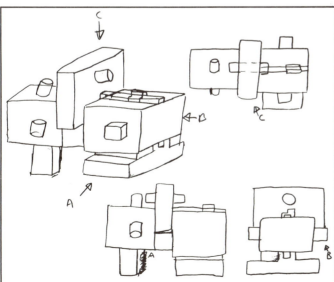

sketches) until a final arrangement was arrived at.

The subsequent stages of this exercise were concerned with translating the idea into a final 'workshop drawing' that would enable the child to realise his design in wood. The first step was to determine the true shape of the various component parts and to relate the separate sketch views. This is the point at which orthographic projection was introduced, and a

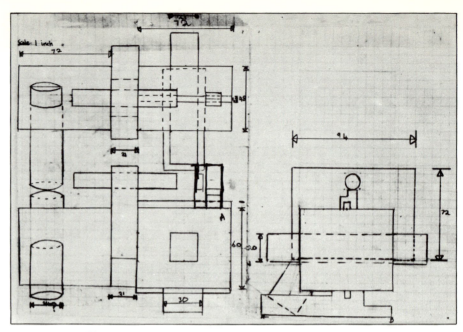

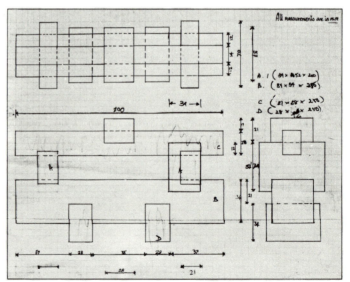

freehand third-angle sketch of the assembly was made. The second step was to consider the practical limitations imposed by the available materials. Prepared timber (to thickness) was used to prevent the final fabrication stage from becoming unnecessarily protracted. This inevitably involved some adjustment in the proportions of the parts which were all resolved in the final 'workshop drawing'. This drawing was made on squared paper so as to speed up its development. To insist on formal technical drawing techniques at this point does nothing to assist the child's progress, and can be a positive hindrance in developing his idea.

The squared paper drawings were then taken into the workshop where they became the basis for a boy's third woodworking exercise. In the first form he will have used a coping saw, touched on the use of a plane, and learned finishing techniques; subsequently he will have added those of marking out with square and gauge, and the use of the tenon saw and chisel. Now he has only to learn to prepare his wood to width and he is able to go ahead with the complete fabrication process. Some designs will need special grooving and slotting techniques, but these are easily covered where needed. Finally, the finish and colour scheme are considered, and this is an exercise in its own right.

Humans are extremely active beings – always thinking, moving and doing. They are the most exciting of all natural forms and there is nothing more stimulating than the study of ourselves. Some aspect of human behaviour is examined at every stage of our course so that the children gain an ever-deepening awareness of what human beings are able to feel, express and achieve. In the second year a study is made of the human body, its proportions and typical postures, as a continuation of the study of proportion and structure begun in the first objective drawing exercises. At this age of 12+, very little consideration is given to anatomical and structural detail. It is characteristic expressions and gestures that fascinate a child of this age and which he will readily explore.

The first and seemingly insuperable difficulty of getting people to look dispassionately at other people can be overcome by engaging the whole class in bizarre and exciting events. Fighting, wrestling matches, disaster scenes, angry crowds; all these and more can be used to overcome this barrier. On occasions we have reached the seemingly ludicrous situation of 15 bodies 'caught' in writhing postures reminiscent of the Laocoön for just five of the group to draw (in 10 minutes)!

Clearly, in these exercises the child is concerned with capturing forms, gestures and emotional expressions, but it is also easy and important to establish the connection between these intertwining, rolling and twisting figures, the more abstract interslotting and sliding of the three-dimensional geometric blocks, and the completeness of the whole that was apparent in the green pepper.

Likewise, these drawings are part of the data-gathering activity in that they can be used as a direct source of ideas for graphic developments, bringing in the use of sources such as magazine illustrations of suitably dramatic, humorous or pathetic situations. In all this work it is the interplay, proportion and juxtaposition of parts in a structural and emotional sense that is our chief concern.

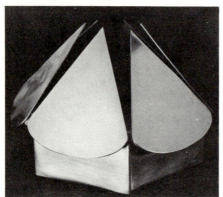

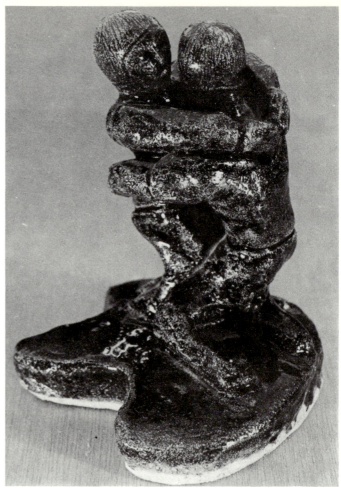

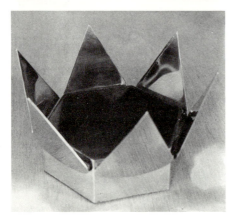

Such excited and deeply felt awareness of form finds direct three-dimensional expression in the modelling of clay figures and bas-relief, and this can either be of the single figure or the interrelated group.

The observational and analytical drawing already described is a fertile source of ideas for every decorative craft. We illustrate the way in which it can be used in conjunction with wire sculpture, etching or cloisonné work techniques and silversmithing.

The manipulation of tinned copper wire forms a very useful introduction to work on a jewellery scale as a direct contrast to the heavier woodwork, metalwork and clay processes. An essential sensitivity and delicacy of touch is achieved by starting out with a straightforward test exercise, say a circle of a given diameter, which sets the child an immediate challenge in terms of skill. Once this is achieved the child is able to develop his own interpretation of the data gathered in the earlier drawing activities. These designs may be two or three-dimensional, and can be further enhanced by the selective additions of tissue paper.

The more stylised developments of fruit, flowers, plants and figures are readily usable as the starting points for jewellery design along the lines of medallions, cloisonné techniques applied to polyester resin plaques and enamelling, etched bowls etc. The production of a successful piece of work requires both a fully organised and developed design, and a high standard of workmanship. The initial stylised drawing is first converted to a full-sized mock-up of the intended product. Often, this cannot be achieved without at least a demonstration of the relevant craft and an explanation of some of the principal limitations of the technique. In the case of cloisonné enamelling, for example, it is almost essential that a complete mock-up is made in card and wire or else the children can easily get into difficulties in the workshop through producing impractical designs.

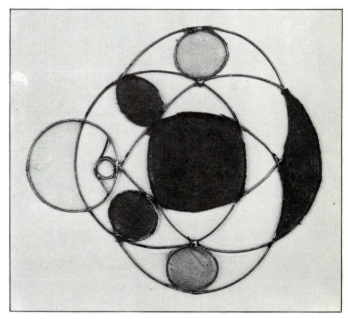

*Nigel Billington and John Jeffery are jointly in charge of the Design Centre at Pocklington School. The school is a direct grant independent boys' day/boarding school. The Design Centre, which opened in January 1970, brought together under one roof an existing Art Department and a new Technical Unit and the course as developed at present is followed by all boys in the 11 to 13 age range. (Approximately 60 to 80 boys are in each year group.)*

*All boys in Forms I, II and III are timetabled to spend two double periods each week in the Centre, one on the art side and the other on the technical, in groups of twenty. The distribution varies from time to time and a group may spend all four periods in one place, or two groups may combine together for a joint session if a particular phase of their work demands it. In the fifth form boys may opt to take art and/or pottery as O-level subjects and continue on to A-level in the sixth form. There are no examinations at present in craft or technical drawing, although technical projects are sometimes offered as part of the sixth-form general studies programme. The present integrated design course will continue up through the school, with the first boys sitting an O-level in Design in 1979. The decision to integrate the main outline of the work has demanded a close collaboration between the teaching staff. Naturally, the* greater the number of people involved in a scheme, the greater the difficulties involved in ensuring common objectives and the co-ordinated activity that enables a single topic to be pursued in a number of different areas. In the light of their experience with part-time teachers, students and schemes with local art and teacher training colleges, they feel that the scale of enterprise is of vital importance in the success of a design department. What they may lose in extensive facilities is more than compensated for by increased cohesion within the unit.*

# Simon Langton
# Grammar School for Boys

## Mike Stevenson

*Mike Stevenson*

*'Designing, and creating ideas and objects gives me great satisfaction. Since my childhood I have always been planning and making things, it is something I have an intuitive feel for; practising my own work seems essential to my survival. Teaching certainly adds a further dimension and gives me the opportunity to pass on this experience to others, and I hope that some may find similar enthusiasm to my own.*

*'The wealth of the subject is reflected in the diversity of approach to its teaching currently practised in schools. I hope that when design comes of age in the national curriculum, this quality will not be lost.*

*'I try at all levels to create a flexible learning situation that fosters motivation and the freedom to explore creatively in the student, yet still manages to fit the constraints and the realities of the real world. Working with people in their formative years, I do recognise that Design cannot be the mainspring of existence to them all, but the need to create and "wrought" objects is a common desire that is basic. So I have no reservations about the place of design in general education.'*

I hope, by giving a description here of work undertaken by one student, to give at the same time an impression of the nature and intention of the department where the project was carried out. The surroundings that make the work possible and the work itself go hand in hand and this particular example emphasises the connection, since the student had no previous experience in design and the course he undertook was new.

A group of five students embarked upon the first sixth-form design course in 1973. The course had two aims: first, to dovetail with the then very new Oxford A-level Design syllabus, and to provide a recognised qualification in the subject; and secondly, to build a successful basic design study which might fit any student who so wished, for direct entry to BA design courses.

The emphasis on design teaching, as distinct from craft work, began in 1971. Prior to 1973, its influence was applied to parts of the lower and middle school only. The new sixth-form course needed the academic respectability provided by the Oxford qualification to run in parallel with other A-levels in the school. It also transpired that had this syllabus not existed, it would have been necessary to create one along similar lines in order to run a broad foundation course for BA direct entry.

Of the first group of students, one – David Harwood – later chose to apply for and obtained the direct entry option. It is his work that is described here.

At his point of entry to the sixth form, he had no previous experience of being taught design. He was good at craft and art, reasonable academically, and had some knowledge of technical drawing. He was selected on his merits to take the course. This procedure still operates, even though there is now a design course in the middle school. It seems a good principle to offer design to students with all types of O-level combinations, for there are those who find they have aptitude but not time to take O-level Design and Technology.

The school is for boys and the traditional place of craft has been taken over by design. There is a strong emphasis on three-dimensional design in the department. It is fair to add that craft work for its own sake is still fostered, especially in the junior years. There is independence from the separate Art Department, but co-operation exists where necessary.

Probably the most coveted facility, and in many ways the most valuable one, is a purpose-built and furnished drawing office/studio for design. This is absolutely essential for working in this subject; a strong emphasis is put on the graphic side of the three-dimensional design activities.

The project around which this case study is centred was second year sixth-form work. A brief guide to the first year may put it into context. Although the aims of the year have not changed greatly since this time, with experience the practice has. The Oxford syllabus, also, has now become more explicit in its expectations.

David Harwood weathered the first year well. His initial design diet was a number of materials-orientated projects in wood, metal, plastics and ceramics. These were aimed at fostering an enquiring approach to the potential and qualities of materials. Experimental workshop practice encourages appreciation of their nature, use and cross reference. Few constraints are applied on what is possible at this stage.

An awareness of industrial as well as craft technologies is encouraged, but not restrictively so, it is hoped. The aim throughout is to develop creativity.

In many ways this part of the work follows college foundation course practice, but throughout there is an awareness that it is solely design that is being served, there being no fine art students. The 'basic design' approach to drawing, colour, structure etc, is used to help develop a means of communication and an understanding of the fundamental points of visual aesthetics and design.

There is no pretence, however, that the same amount of time, facilities, and range of in-depth expertise can be devoted to the work as in the colleges. It is early for feedback to be complete, but it seems that talented students are not the worse for doing the work at school, thus gaining a year, but this might be thought to be a controversial issue.

During the first year, then, a number of facts are established. As great a range of foundation studies is covered as can be squeezed into the time available. It is hoped, too, that students can begin to lend a personal style and approach to their work. Emphases develop both from the student and from the teacher.

For example, set reading and analysis work seek to point out that many design situations, especially those met commercially, do not in fact cater for real needs. The notion of social responsibility through design is emphasised. It is not perhaps possible, in later life, to be so idealistic. At this stage it seems to be a more mature expression than, say, 'truth to materials' or 'fitness for purpose'. These notions of aesthetic rightness can be a little introverted and self-indulgent and must seem to a student to foster aloofness from real problems.

In addition, although a student project, it is most important, in my view, that a situation should be created in which a real innovation can be made – not a creative fantasy, but one capable of fitting realistic constraints. In this way a number of exciting ideas have been generated and proved that are worthy of patent.

Apart from these provisos, the choice of topic is almost unlimited. The restrictions imposed by facilities have not really prevented any student from developing a theme. So far, we have over-stepped the limitations occasionally, but with outside co-operation we have avoided disaster. It seems that, with enthusiasm, helpful contacts can be found easily, thus proving the value of an examination where the student nominates his own topic.

Against this background, David drew on personal experience. His mother's involvement with a playgroup meant that he was used to hearing about mothers' problems in transporting young children.

A visit to the group soon suggested that prams and pushchairs came in a vast assortment of constructions, configurations and materials – and all were the subject of a lot of valid criticism by their owners.

It was here, too, that the first mistake of the project was made – that of lack of reportage. Just a few negatives, sketches and notes of the things that inspired its choice would have been of value. Not much is missed later in analysing equipment and opinions, but the situation that crystallised the project idea would be of documentary value.

Having made a decision about the theme, David was encouraged to anticipate a possible run and outcome of the brief. This ensures that adequate scope exists for ideas; helps to determine objectives; helps to plan the use of time; and

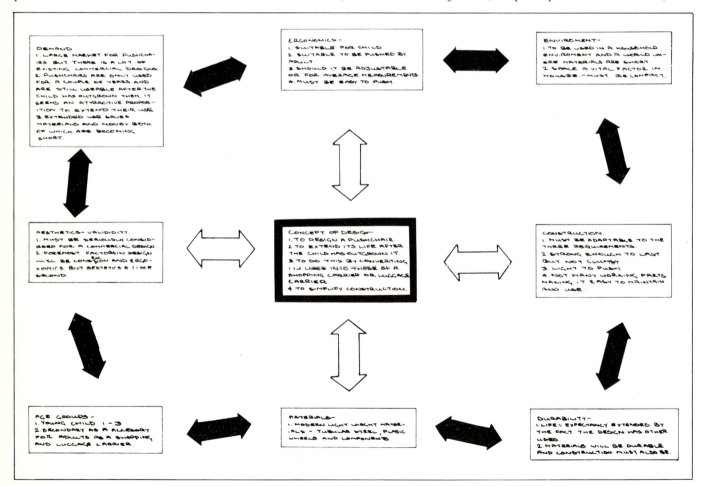

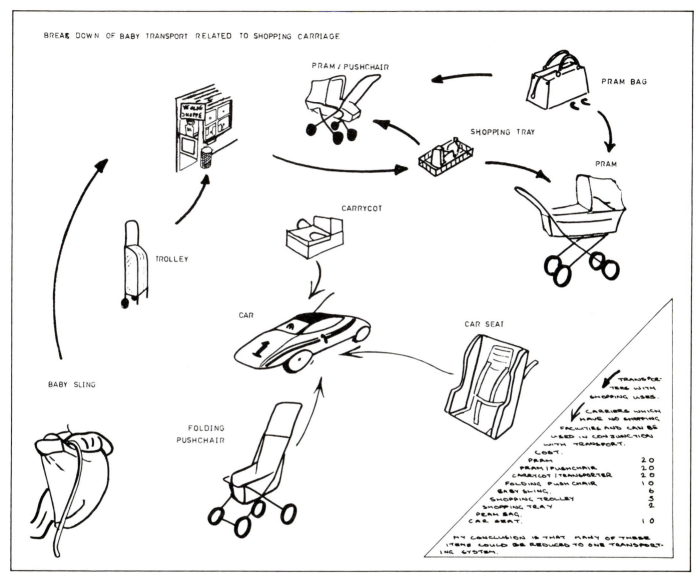

PRAM / PUSHCHAIR

PRAM BAG

SHOPPING TRAY

PRAM

CARRYCOT

TROLLEY

CAR

CAR SEAT

BABY SLING

FOLDING
PUSHCHAIR

TRANSPORTERS WITH SHOPPING USES.

CARRIERS WHICH HAVE NO SHOPPING FACILITIES AND CAN BE USED IN CONJUNCTION WITH TRANSPORT.

COST.

| | |
|---|---|
| PRAM | 20 |
| PRAM / PUSHCHAIR | 20 |
| CARRYCOT / TRANSPORTER | 20 |
| FOLDING PUSH CHAIR | 10 |
| BABY SLING. | 6 |
| SHOPPING TROLLEY | 5 |
| SHOPPING TRAY | 2 |
| PRAM BAG. | |
| CAR SEAT. | 10 |

MY CONCLUSION IS THAT MANY OF THESE ITEMS COULD BE REDUCED TO ONE TRANSPORTING SYSTEM.

makes a student responsible for his own actions. This planning procedure has led to other students rejecting themes and finding better ones. It also ensures that there will be a defined structure to research, since there is often a temptation to deviate from the main objective.

A planning chart was produced, which was supposed to ensure that the project kept on schedule. It did not, but without the chart the situation might have been much worse! The teacher can be of great help in giving advice about this detail planning for, knowing the student's capacity for work, he can ensure that the week-to-week aims can be achieved. David's problem was one that was not unpleasant to correct:

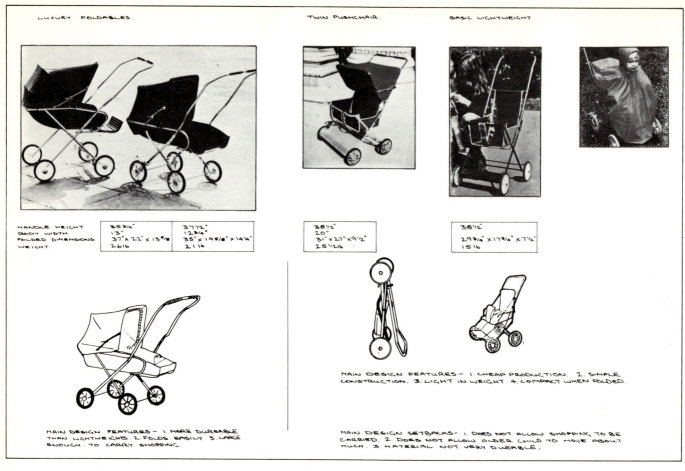

| | | | | |
|---|---|---|---|---|
| HANDLE HEIGHT | 35¾" | 37½" | 38½" | 38½" |
| BODY WIDTH | 13" | 12¾" | 20" | |
| FOLDED DIMENSIONS | 37" x 22" x 13⅝" | 35" x 19⅝" x 14¼" | 31" x 27" x 9½" | 29¾" x 17¾" x 7½" |
| WEIGHT. | 26 lb | 21 lb | 25½ lb | 15 lb |

MAIN DESIGN FEATURES - 1. CHEAP PRODUCTION. 2. SIMPLE CONSTRUCTION. 3. LIGHT IN WEIGHT 4. COMPACT WHEN FOLDED.

MAIN DESIGN FEATURES - 1. MORE DURABLE THAN LIGHTWEIGHTS. 2. FOLDS EASILY 3. LARGE ENOUGH TO CARRY SHOPPING.

MAIN DESIGN SETBACKS - 1. DOES NOT ALLOW SHOPPING TO BE CARRIED. 2. DOES NOT ALLOW OLDER CHILD TO MOVE ABOUT MUCH. 3. MATERIAL NOT VERY DURABLE.

*Above: worksheet showing investigation of commercial pushchairs.*

*Right: worksheet showing a 'typical' commercial pushchair as part of the design investigation.*

he enjoyed his research too much and became more deeply involved with some aspects than was healthy, time being at a premium. This did not damage the project, but in later stages emphasis deviated from the original intentions. More became known about the users' problems; fewer details about the physical solution were proved. Rigid adherence to the planning chart might perhaps have prevented this, but it would have diluted David's personal approach, since he was not obsessed with absolute engineering detail.

The first task he set himself at this stage was to clarify his brief by trying to establish the main uses to which a pram/pushchair was put. There were baffling options presented to mothers. These ranged from baby or toddler's carriages, which seemed to be designed in an age gone by, to the baby buggy that was so minimal that it seemed to be a wheeled extension of the child.

The information-gathering foray began by collecting catalogues and specifications to see if manufacturers (surely they have the solution?) really knew their business. David's first project report stated with hindsight: 'With any project

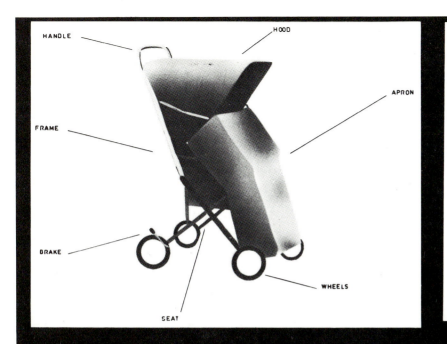

HANDLE     HOOD

APRON

FRAME

BRAKE

WHEELS

SEAT

Handle

The handle should be the correct height for
the user. Most models have handles about
36 inches high (see ergonomic studies).
The handle should also be easy to hold and
push so that the pushchair can be properly
controled.
Handle grips should ensure that the hand is
kept comfortable and can grip tightly.

Hood and apron

This is a vital piece of equipment for the
light weight. Some models donot include
these features.
A young child has to be protected from the
elements but manufactures seem to think that
cost is more important for promoting thier
products.

Seat

It must be made of materials which can with-
stand heavy wear, be easily cleaned and are
waterproof. The seat must give a ceartain amount of protection to the child. Some seat have safety straps which hold the child secur-
ely and all have a crutch strap. It has to be
adjustable to hold a child for two or three
years in its development.

Wheels

Many models have polypropelene wheels. The baby buggy has double wheels which become loose
easily. Wheels last but tyres wear quickly and
need to be replaced. The axle ajcining the rear wheels is not always very strong.

Brake

Is the brake sufficient to hold the pushchair
and occupant? Most models have a two wheel hand
brake which seems to be adequate. Brake levers
are not always strong and are liable to fall off
Some levers are hard to find which can be dangerous. Mechanism can be a hazard for childrens
fingers.

Frame

A light weight frame should also be strong.
Most are made of chrome or are painted metal.
The folding mechanism should be easy to use,
but not so easy that it folds with the child
in it. This is what the baby buggy is liable
to do.
The joints are often dangerous for small children who may catch their fingers.

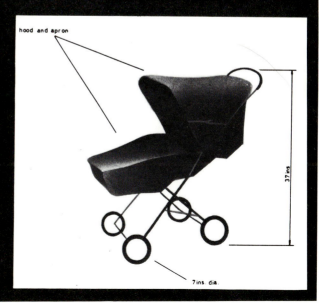

hood and apron

37 ins

7ins. dia.

of this nature, collecting information can be difficult. Pushchair manufacturers will supply catalogues, but these are of limited use.' He hoped, naively perhaps, to find some common thread of intention, but the only one found seemed to be commercial. 'Because manufacturers are out to make money, they often forget the real needs of their customers, who in turn forget their own real needs.' There was certainly no coherent approach to users' problems and David acquired a healthy scepticism. He pointed out the way in which the products of some firms played on the natural pride a mother has in her child. He found the luxury market for chrome trim and rose patterns abhorrent. 'A luxury product is usually something which everyone wants, but nobody needs.'

He analysed the manufacturers' psychology in the sales area. There were many of the undesirable factors found in the motor industry, such as planned obsolescence, but none of the compulsory standards of design and construction of that industry.

Safety was felt to be the overriding concern when designing for vulnerable infants. He felt that manufacturers, for various reasons, thought that safety was a poor selling angle and steered clear of it. David needed a way to rationalise the commercial products into some useful statement. He did so in a number of ways.

Charts were produced that listed dimensions and general design features. This gave useful information for reference, especially later, for example to check his own findings about anthropometric data. Drawings were made to show good and bad points in proprietary designs, to compare with the claims in the catalogues. Poor durability was illustrated by photographs of abandoned prams on rubbish tips.

The standard of design and construction was summed up graphically with two 'identi-kit' airbrush drawings, showing the typical pushchair and pram.

In terms of aiding design ideas, these worksheets provided a most important reference and helped more than his written reportage and argument to sum up the current commercial state of affairs.

The graphic work produced during this phase matured rapidly. David experimented with various media and laid the foundations that enabled the illustration of ideas in later stages. His approach to graphics did not stagnate, although pressure of time later on led to the adoption of more rapid methods and the airbrush, for example, had to be abandoned. It was the exploratory stages that yielded the best graphic

work. In the final solution area of the project, worksheets became a kind of shorthand, lacking in objectivity. Although by this stage David had opted to use his sketchbook as the main method of expressing ideas, in it there was no compromise and the standard of drawing improved until its close.

The next inquiry stage was user-based. There were two

*'The end of the road!' From a section on planned obsolescence – a study of manufacturers' standards of construction and users' attitudes to the product.*

distinct interests – the mother's and the child's – but naturally they overlapped. David took the mother's subjective interests first. What was she likely to be doing when she had need of special transport for junior apart from simply moving along? This is the list in his report section 'My concept of a pushchair':

1 Shopping
2 Getting on and off buses/trains, in and out of cars etc
3 Travelling in busy areas
4 Travelling over rough surfaces and up and down kerbs
5 Transporting and parking an active, attention-seeking child

He was aware that satisfying all 'in-the-field situations' would not be easy: 'The point that a pushchair can adapt to as many different situations as possible is difficult to develop, because in doing so the design becomes too much of a compromise. The transporter has to be purposely designed to suit the situations it is most likely to meet, with as few additional aids as possible, but to clarify his criteria he added that 'The design has to revolve around safety, which is most important, compactability (sic), lightness and durability; but with these four points we have many more which are part and parcel of them, or contradict them. A cheap, hard-wearing, shopping-carrying, small-sized push-chair sounds very good, but each feature would be too compromised.'

He recognised also that the pushchair has more than one interface with other systems and enlarged on this, saying 'If the pushchair is to fulfil its role more fully, it either has to adapt itself or the system has to be adapted for it'.

At this point the project could have diverged from its original aims, leading to recommendations about 'push-on buses' and other adaptations to present transport hardware. The temptation was resisted, but it seemed to be a valid path – why have a folding pushchair to get on a bus; why not re design the bus?

David stuck rigidly to his brief to produce a pushchair within the existing accepted definition. This is not to say that he did not allow himself a few peripheral distractions. He made sketches for various developments – a battery-powered buggy for mother and child, monorail baby transport systems, pedal pushchairs, and so on. 'If we ever get to the stage where motorised baby and child transporters are common, we are in trouble, because obviously all other members of the community will have their personal transporters. Anyway, pushing a pushchair does the average housewife more good than harm, helping to reduce the amount of middle age spread.'

David's ideas about concept and configuration now required the interaction of field experience that only a chat with mothers could provide. 'The most important aspect of research is the practical information that can be gained from the public.' He was acutely aware that it is better to be uninformed than ill-informed. 'A great many problems are met in all stages of a questionnaire. The first is deciding what you really want to know and how you should convey it on the questionnaire. The wording of the questions must be kept on a level which everyone will understand, but simple yes/no answers are not always satisfactory. My mother, who is involved with a local playgroup, disposed of nearly twenty copies. Of these she got back half. This relative success was due to the fact that the people my mother gave the questionnaires to came in contact with her almost daily, thus collection was fairly simple. An interesting point was that some people gave a great deal of extra information, while others gave only the bare essentials, but if the questionnaire was properly laid out, the bare essentials should be enough. Obviously I have to find how to reach a larger amount of pushchair-pushing people.'

Questions in the survey covered a number of matters: when and why a pushchair was used; its interrelation to other transport systems; any accidents, such as tipping over; and structural and detail design criticisms. Child-centred observations asked for age, subjective data related to comfort and whether it was possible for the child to sleep in the chair properly, for example.

David had expected much from his questionnaire results. Although the information was useful it did not – as he had, I think, imagined – lead to the consumers 'designing' the product for him. They knew what they wanted, but their requirements reflected the many contradictions mentioned earlier in the search for the ideal concept and configuration. The questionnaire simply added essential detail, reinforcing David's own observations. 'For example, I noticed that some pushchairs were prone to tip up and this observation was clarified by the results of the questionnaire. Once I realised the problems, it was pointless to continue with this kind of research, because all it was doing was stagnating any creative or practical ideas I had evolved.'

Research 'in the field' was almost finished, but it would be incomplete without considering 'junior's criterion'. David thought it would be fun to project himself into the situation met by the real user. The result is a diversion, identifying real problems hardly catered for in existing situations. The project report passage is called 'Keep still, little George'.

'Small children are liable to become very restless when they are being pushed around from one shop to another. As well as being annoying for mother and child, it is rather a dangerous situation. If the mother's attention is not distracted, she can perform the job of pushing much more efficiently and safely. Apart from wrapping anchor chains around little George or giving him a shot of sedative, there are few satisfactory ways of restraining him.'

'Play is a natural process by which children gain experience of life. So why should we cut out this process while the child is in the pushchair? Unfortunately play can be quite an active pastime, so that any play which is introduced must be of a more sedentary nature. Also, once the child has gained its experience from the plaything, the child will lose interest and start to become restless. To entertain the child is not enough, because this only encourages more restless tendencies and a child who is always entertained never learns to entertain itself. The emphasis must be on occupation, not entertainment, but to keep a two-year-old occupied for any length of time is a difficult business.'

'Because the pushchair is on the move it would be frustrating for the child to try to draw or paint. Also, bored kids might have a tendency to drop their pens and pencils into the road. There must be some choice for the child, so that if boredom does set in, there is always an alternative pastime. The space which the games, etc take up must also be carefully considered, so as not to add to the burden of the already overworked mother.'

Further reasoning is provided about 'in-pram entertainment', but the most lively expressions on this topic are some fantastic ideas shown in drawings of the 'telly pushchair' and 'football' chair.

There were at this stage some gaps in David's knowledge about 'junior'. He still had no data about the dimensions of a growing baby. He could find no published anthropometric data covering the age ranges compatible with pushchair usage. It would be dangerous to take the information from manufacturers' products; they had been a less than satisfactory source on some other points of design.

This was yet another reason to go out and get information. First a period was spent in the studio, designing a device to measure babies and toddlers. With hindsight it seems that too many alternative devices were formulated, time was wasted and too many excellent, precise worksheets were produced. It might have been better to advance with just a tape measure, but because variables were few, David relished the situation – it was such a contrast to the major problem. The work was well illustrated graphically, resulting in the production of a set of maximum, minimum and average dimensions on which later work could draw.

The project progressed to the design stage. Research did not totally cease, but it was easier to define what information

*Above: 'In-pram entertainment' from 'Keep still, little George', a section from the project report.*

*Right: the final solution reached for the child-measuring chair. 'In use its shape was rather frightening to the sitters.'*

was wanted. Findings were used to solve detail problems associated with producing a material solution.

Any field of human activity where advances are made through what can be called design in its broadest sense, from the frontiers of physics to primitive solutions to age-old problems, requires three basic ingredients: the ability to extrapolate (by definition, the creative function), skill and knowledge. It is not sufficient for school design work to emphasise research, reportage and creative fantasy alone. There must be the validating factors of a technology and skill. Naturally, there will be a particular emphasis in each case, but this should not be to the exclusion of any of the three factors.

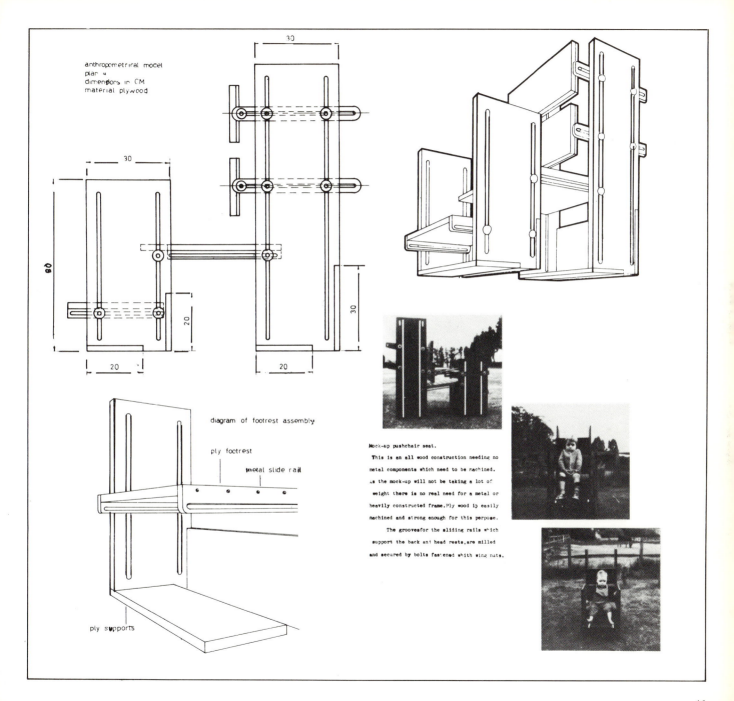

anthropometrical model
plan 4
dimensions in CM
material plywood

30

30

60

20

30

20

20

diagram of footrest assembly

ply footrest

metal slide rail

ply supports

Mock-up pushchair seat.

This is an all wood construction needing no
metal components which need to be machined.
As the mock-up will not be taking a lot of
weight there is no real need for a metal or
heavily constructed frame. Ply wood is easily
machined and strong enough for this purpose.

The grooves for the sliding rails which
support the back and head rests, are milled
and secured by bolts fastened whith wing nuts.

41

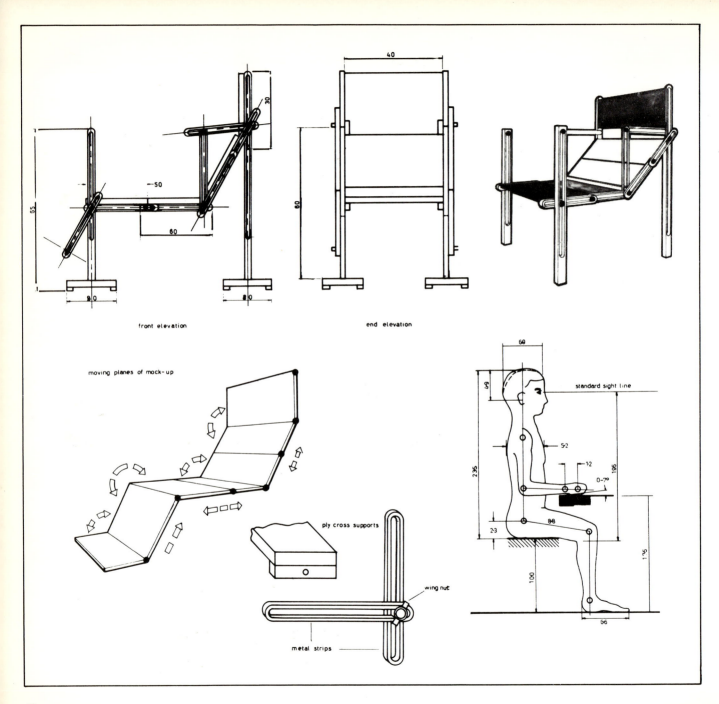

front elevation

end elevation

moving planes of mock-up

ply cross supports

wing nut

metal strips

standard sight line

*Left: 'Measurements for the average pushchair were obtained using the test chair.'*

*Right: a general configuration investigation based on mothers' needs without reference to construction.*
'These designs show some of the problems encountered when a system for holding shopping is incorporated in the design. A shopping bag attached to the pushchair takes up a lot of room and has to be folded up with the pushchair, which means that shopping has to be transferred to another bag. The ideal shopping carrier is one which carries the shopping bag itself. A shopping tray is one solution but this has the disadvantage of being close to the ground and existing designs have to be removed before the pushchair can be folded. The shopping carrier must be an integral part of the design and not just an afterthought, as is very much the case with existing designs which are likely to tip up when any quantity of shopping is carried.'

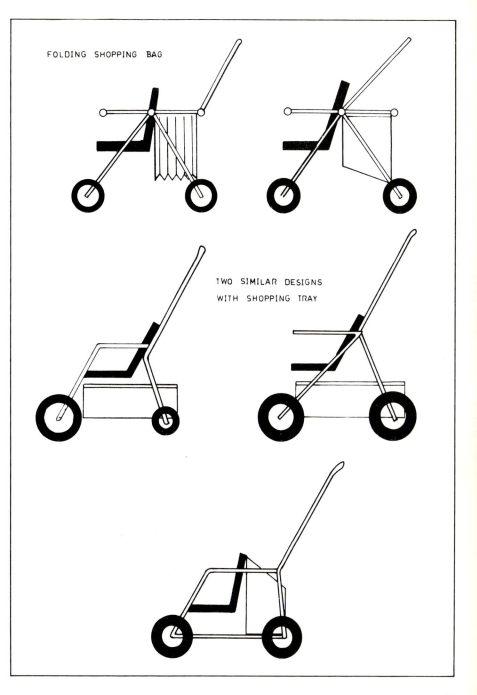

FOLDING SHOPPING BAG

TWO SIMILAR DESIGNS
WITH SHOPPING TRAY

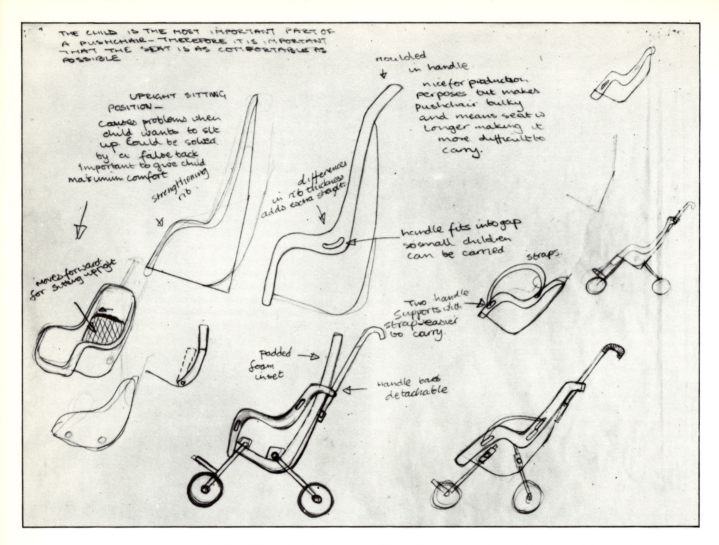

THE CHILD IS THE MOST IMPORTANT PART OF A PUSHCHAIR — THEREFORE IT IS IMPORTANT THAT THE SEAT IS AS COMFORTABLE AS POSSIBLE

UPRIGHT SITTING POSITION — causes problems when child wants to sit up. Could be solved by a false back. Important to give child maximum comfort

strengthening rib

moves forward for sitting upright

differences in rib thickness adds extra strength.

moulded in handle nice for production perposes but makes pushchair bulky and means seat is longer making it more difficult to carry.

handle fits into gap so small children can be carried

Two handle supports with strap — easier to carry.

straps.

padded foam inset

Handle bars detachable

It was quite natural, therefore, that David's project became orientated towards materials and technology, which would enable him to recommend a solution. Design science – ergonomic and anthropometric work – became important, as did studies of such things as structure, configuration, safety factors and industrial economics.

His earlier graphic studies of particular problems, the statements in the project report as to the order and importance of certain factors, were the skeleton on which he was to build.

The only way to evaluate this stage of the work is to thumb through David's sketchbook. The balance and equation of these factors was constantly reviewed and extrapolated until a solution began to emerge. Above all other criteria, however, it was the validity of the suggested design in terms of the prevailing production technologies that was important. I am not saying this is always the case; other projects at this level had other emphases. The pushchair, however, is a mass-market commodity and has to be competitive with its rivals.

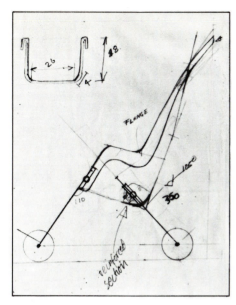

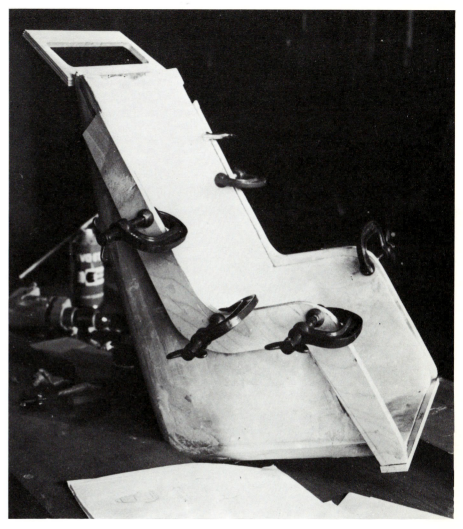

*Above and left: 'Research suggests a pushchair that is essentially a light seat made of polypropylene with detachable or retractable wheels. The seat and child can then be either carried, wheeled or strapped in a car.'*

*Right: the model was constructed using aluminium, wood and polyester.*

If it cannot be manufactured competitively, then the design is less valid.

This factor need not present a problem in a school project. Whenever size, cost and facilities are liable to be out of reach, models can lead to quite valid solutions. It is, after all, a method of expression often used by designers to impress ideas on clients.

It is important, however, that models do something more than produce a visual of the solution; a drawing can do that. In

David's case it enabled detailed features to be designed and proved as the model progressed.

His design for the seat shape was intended to be produced in lightweight polypropylene. The pushchair is a monocoque construction; the seat carries wheels, when fitted, and child. Although it would be necessary to spend thousands of pounds to tool for his design in the intended material, by observing other polypropylene chair shells, he was able to model the stresses likely to be met. So a grp or aluminium fabrication

*The seat with wheels and struts removed, as used in a car. The carrying straps and harness can be seen.*

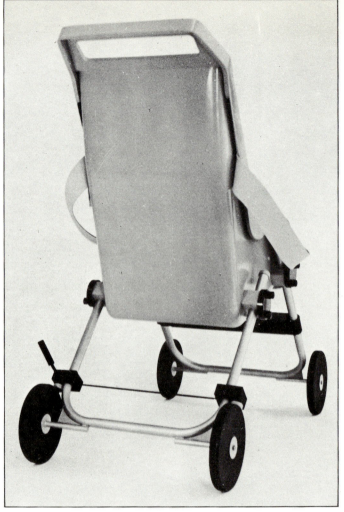

was adequate in this case for the seat. The all-important anthropometric recommendations were tested, and the design features, such as fitted cushions for the younger age range, were experimented with. In addition, the chair was tried in other modes – for carrying, as a car seat, and as a high chair – and so in this case all features of the model were built to take the full stresses of use where possible.

When considering both final design and model, reaching an 'ultimate' solution in terms of absolute technical detail, espe-cially at the cost of time better spent in the type of research featured earlier, is a naïve goal. Often new materials and technologies can render such solutions obsolete or inappro-priate shortly after their conception. These are surely the domain of professional designers and industry – awareness, not obsession, being the validating factor. I think that this study proves the point, for the ideas are not diminished by being produced in model form. It should be emphasised that the design and production of most items today are team work

*Left and below: the finished model in the pushchair mode. Wheels and support adjust to give different seat heights and angles. The clamps can be swivelled to allow the wheels to be retracted. The brake is integral with the rear strut and axle assembly. The foot-rest clips to its supporting struts and is also adjustable for height.*

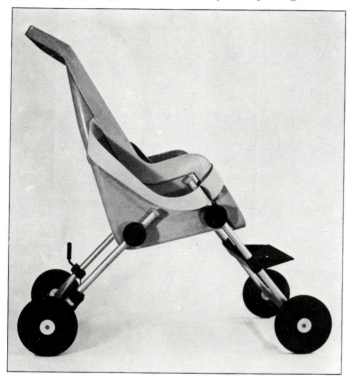

reviewed with hindsight. It is of significance to both student and teacher for all these reasons, but in terms of learning and experience, it is not arriving but making the journey that is of lasting value to the student.

*Mike Stevenson is Head of the Design Department at Simon Langton Grammar School for Boys, Canterbury, which has 600 pupils and has a three-stream entry. There are facilities for wood, metal, plastics and ceramics work and a drawing studio/office, the overall space totalling 380 square metres. There is a basic craft introduction to various materials in the lower school, plus teaching in drawing. Years 1 to 4 have two periods per week in the area, the teacher to pupil ratio being generally 1:16 at this level. Increasing emphasis on design and graphic literacy is made in the middle school as materials technologies are learned. An option to specialise is made at the end of the fourth year, then five periods per week may be devoted to London University O-level Design and Technology and/or O-level Geometric and Engineering Drawing. The sixth-form course is as described; seven periods per week and any available free time is devoted to it. The department seeks to offer a general and basic course in the subject to prepare students for work at tertiary level in both arts and science fields, through Oxford A-level Design.*

and few individuals can produce a complete and detailed solution on their own.

The finished artefact, being fairly permanent, is an important realisation of a stage reached but, like any aspect of educational work, it is merely an expression of the level of understanding at one point in time. In the design context it shows both faults and strengths in the ideas that formed it. Additionally, it can give great satisfaction to the maker in its own right. Through achieving a goal, it is cherished and can be

# Manshead School

## Phil Mason

*Phil Mason*

'Clothing, furniture, tools, magazines, advertising, houses, schools, civic centres, road systems, timetables – all these and much more represent the designed world with which we are surrounded. Wherever civilisation has made its mark, man's creative energy is evident through the artefacts, architecture and pictorial expressions that he has left behind. In an age of automation and mechanised mass-production it is all too easy to disregard man's inner creative drive, which has led him to shape his environment since the dawn of history.

'Creative expression is a key factor in human experience. In education this area of human endeavour has often been undervalued, especially during the period of secondary schooling. Sound education through creative experience in the use of materials is concerned with the formation and expression of ideas and the realisation of thoughts and feelings. Design is as intrinsic a part of our culture as the spoken or written word and the logical reasoning of the scientist or mathematician. If one accepts the axiom that education is the preparation for life itself, then clearly design activity must have a fundamental place in the curriculum structure, if future generations are to develop a critical awareness of their surroundings and a responsibility to the environment they will inhabit.'

Over the past decade or so, a clear philosophy of design education has emerged, centred on the creative development of the individual pupil in relation to this natural and man-made environment. Through design education it is hoped that pupils will become aware of and sensitive to their responsibility as members of society for the man-made environment in which they live. Everything that is designed affects the quality of human lives to a greater or lesser extent, for better or worse, and nobody can insulate himself from the designed world. It is therefore vital that children should be exposed to experiences in their formal education that will develop an appreciation of design. It would seem logical that the most effective way to stimulate such attitudes is by participation in design activity. However, it should be clearly stated that the aim of design education is not to make all pupils into first or second-rate designers, although it is hoped that some will attain a high standard, but to use design activity as a generally formative educational experience.

This account is a case study of a particular project developed in an upper school design faculty. It is essentially a descriptive narrative and does not claim to be unique either in situation or in approach. One hopes that through a record of the structure, organisation and experiences of both teachers and pupils, a picture of a practical application of some of the concepts of design education will emerge.

A number of pupils were asked to write a few lines about the projects with which they were engaged, stating problems from which they set out to find design solutions. These comments have been used to punctuate the photographs appearing with this text, which covers case studies of pupils at work developing ideas, making and testing their designs.

Much of the work with senior pupils in design departments has aimed at placing pupils in a role that is parallel to that of the professional designer. However, the majority of situations schools can offer are simulations and often lack realism because designing has taken place in an academic vacuum, whereas the work of the professional designer is geared towards the needs of a client and the solution of his problems. The professional designer might well envy the school design situation. Indeed, if more designers were given the sort of freedom many teachers give their pupils, our designed environment might be functionally, visually and socially less depressing. But the designer is usually constrained to work on projects that are acceptable to market trends, 'popular' taste and the pre-conceived ideas and conditions dictated to him by his paymaster.

It was the opportunity to link the work of pupils more closely to real life – the needs and restrictions of a client – which led to the adoption of the project to be described on the following pages.

Manshead School is a purpose-built upper school of approximately 1,100 pupils aged 13 to 18 years, on the southern outskirts of Dunstable. It occupies a campus site with two other schools – St Mary's Lower School (4 to 9 years) and Streetfield Middle School (9 to 13 years), which has recently opened. The Design Faculty at Manshead is situated in a purpose-built, partially open-plan block. During the six years since the school was re-organised from the former Dunstable Grammar School, practical work has been strongly orientated towards a philosophy of design education. An integrated course forms the core of the activities within the Faculty and leads to Mode 3 Examinations of the East Anglian Examinations Board. Since the introduction of the Combined Craft and Design Syllabus a thematic approach has been used from which pupils have developed their own project briefs. Experience has shown that some starting points are more successful than others and topics have ranged from the highly functional, such as 'Tables and Tableware', to open abstract topics – such as 'Modules and Units'.

The search for the next year's theme starts as soon as the academic year begins, and over the succeeding months various ideas are discussed, rejected or noted for reference. A major problem with this thematic approach has been finding a topic that can be freely interpreted by pupils working in a wide variety of media, including graphics, printmaking, ceramics, wood, metal, plastics and textiles. Despite this the team has persevered with this approach as a starting point for the development of design briefs. We have done this to prevent a fragmentation often seen within design departments where in practice work often becomes a mere sampling of different practical activities. Our aim has been the integration of aesthetic, technical and social awareness.

When a colleague tentatively suggested a project theme based on the needs of young children, its potential was soon apparent. The ready accessibility of a large number of four to nine-year-old children on the campus at St Mary's Lower School meant that our pupils would be able to observe, take measurements, and test prototypes in real life rather than in a simulated situation. The fact that the children of the lower school would become the 'clients' of our pupil designers would add a dimension to this project that had been lacking with previous themes, where it was normal for the evaluation of designs to be a critical discussion between pupil and teacher and a written assessment of its success or failure for the benefit of the CSE moderator.

Following the conception of the project, meetings were initiated between the course team and our lower-school colleagues. First an approach was made to the lower-school headmaster at head of faculty level. Fortunately he too was able to see its potential and was able to assure us of his encouragement and co-operation. It was vital that colleagues from both schools should share a common understanding of the aims and implications of the proposed scheme and a meeting was arranged between the members of the design team and the staff of the lower school. Our lower-school colleagues needed information about the structure and objectives of the course. They needed guidance on such aspects as whether or not they should give help to our pupils in the formulation of design briefs. It was our objective that pupils should seek out the situations that posed problems rather than being told the needs of young children. We felt that the lower-school staff should restrain themselves from suggesting their own solutions when they could see instances where a design might be ineffective or could be improved if tackled differently. Such assistance would be more appropriate after the mock-up or prototype stage, when the pupils' initial ideas could be discussed critically.

The lower-school staff needed to be reassured that their teaching programme would not seriously suffer, nor routines be disrupted due to the constant intrusion of large numbers of adolescents. Also it was felt that some of our pupils might look upon visits to the lower school as an opportunity to dodge work, so a system of supervision was agreed and all pupils were to report to the lower-school office telling the secretary on each visit the exact nature of their business. It was decided that, where possible, pupils should be encouraged to develop a relationship with a particular class and its teacher, who could follow the progress of particular designs.

Past experience with our Combined Crafts and Design Course has shown that the introduction of the theme is of vital importance to the future success of the project. During this period one aims to fire the enthusiasm and imagination, to convey vital information and to set the scene in general. A number of introductory lessons were organised under the heading 'Children at work and play', comprising talks, visits and observations. At some stages all 80 boys and girls came together as a complete group, but at other times they were divided into more intimate units. At the first lesson the topic

*'In his talk Mr Clarke (Headmaster of St Mary's) told us that young children enjoy playing at being adults, so I thought it would be a good idea to build the children a play-house. I talked to the children and they thought it was a good idea too.'*

was explained to the children and the structure and organisation of the course was revealed by the teaching team, as it was felt essential that pupils should fully understand the goals of the course. The next session was a talk by the headmaster of St Mary's Lower School to the complete group in which he was able to explain how the organisation of his school reflected behaviour patterns in young children. He was also able to advise our pupils how to approach young children and to develop their confidence.

The initial talks were followed by a series of afternoon visits by our pupils to St Mary's in small groups. They were given a choice of the age group they were to observe and they were briefed to record, as unobtrusively as possible, children engaged in normal activities – structured teaching situations, breaks in the playground, getting ready at home time etc. From these observations it was hoped that pupils would visualise areas for the potential development of design projects. It was essential that such visits should be in small groups so as not to intrude upon the normal atmosphere of the class and divert the children's attention. While this cycle of group visits was taking place more talks and discussion groups were organised at the upper school. These included topics such as the 'Nature of Design', and techniques for recording ideas and analysing information. A health visitor spoke about safety requirements for equipment designed for young children and illustrated potential hazards. The leader of a Council adventure playground in Stevenage and his assistant described their experiences in providing children's activities using primitive materials during the summer holiday.

During these initial weeks out, pupils were outwardly passive for much of the time, but one hoped that their minds were being stimulated as they were immersed more fully into the project theme. This period was followed by the development of design briefs in which observed situations were translated into problems requiring action. In many instances a four-way dialogue began between pupil designers, design staff, class teachers from the lower school and the lower-school children.

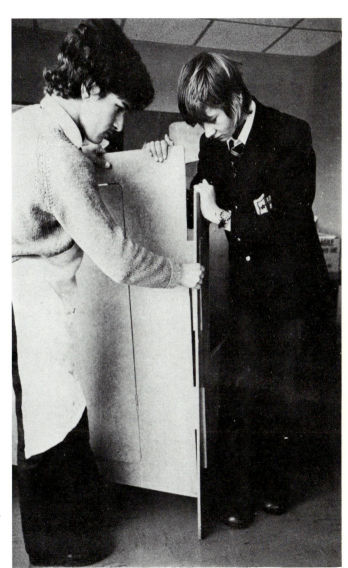

Left: 'I have seen Wendy houses that are hinged at the corner, but I think the hinges can be dangerous as children could trap their fingers. I experimented with panels that could be slotted together and made some models.'

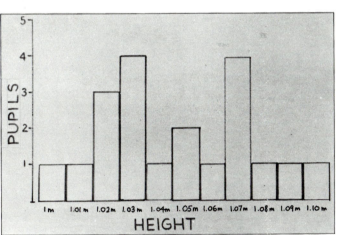

Above: 'The height of the doors and windows had to be in proportion to the children, so I measured all the boys and girls in the class. Then I put their heights on to a graph. There was more variation in height than I had expected.'

Right: 'When I was making the slots I wondered whether they would fit together as well on the full-size house as they did on the model.' 'I took the play-house across to St Mary's with a friend and set it up in the classroom to see what the children thought of it.'

'I asked the children to draw a picture of what the play-house should look like when it was painted. Some wanted bricks and most of them wanted a fence and flowers painted on the outside. They liked bright colours such as red, blue and green. Now I am screen printing the curtains and then I will have to make the furniture. The curtain design is based on the four walls of the play-house fitting together, but when I showed it to the children they said the pattern looked like flowers.'

'The children all liked the play-house and wanted to play in it. Some of them made suggestions for what should go into the house. When I had first been to the school to measure the children they had been shy, but now they were used to me they talked much better.'

*'Mary and I decided to make a puppet theatre because small children like making up stories and if they have got puppets they can act the stories out. We made wooden frames for the sides and they are going to be covered with cloth which will be screen printed. The front is made of hardboard strengthened by a frame. After we had made the theatre we went to St Mary's to see what sort of puppets they wanted and to measure their hands. Some said they would like a crocodile puppet best. When we took the theatre to St Mary's the children seemed very happy and they picked up the puppets and worked them with their hands.'*

There appeared to be three categories of pupil response. First, there were those who were able to formulate a design brief on the basis of their observations of the young children and their lower-school environment. Second, there were those who were more tentative but responded to guidance into situations from which ideas could germinate. For example, 'It takes five minutes for five-year-old children to get their shirts and cardigans on after games', prompted some girls to look into the design of clothing without buttons and play equipment for encouraging manual dexterity similar to that required for the doing-up of buttons. Finally, there were those, a few, who appeared to have little imagination or enthusiasm for developing their own ideas. Here the approach was 'Can you design us some equipment so that we can teach our children about road safety?' This led to the construction of some simple 'soap-box' cars and a road-way system painted onto the playground with such features as pedestrian crossings, and road signs.

The initial choice of projects was very diverse, but there was a distinct tendency for pupils to design items for the younger lower-school children rather than for the older age range. Having observed the infants engrossed in informal play, it was perhaps not surprising that our pupils should attempt to create design briefs around fantasy situations. It was obvious that their own memories of imaginary play were still powerful and production was soon under way on such items as child-sized tanks, space-ships and motor cars. A fantasy theme for the older age group emerged in the form of equipment for dramatic expression, which appealed to several of our pupil designers. A number made puppets in a variety of costumes which gave the young children scope to make up their own plays and stories. Two theatres, one for hand puppets and the other for string puppets, were also constructed.

'One of us noticed when we were watching the younger children in the playground that they often fell down when playing games, so a group of us decided to make some equipment that would help the young children improve their balance. We needed to find out how big their feet were, so one of us made a measuring gauge like they use in shoe shops. Then we made two pairs of stilts, one designed in wood and the other in wood and metal. We made the foot blocks adjustable so that they could be as low as possible when the children started to balance on them.'

'Another thing we made was an adjustable beam that tapers. The height of this can be altered, and it also tilts to different angles so that children can learn to balance going up or down hill.'

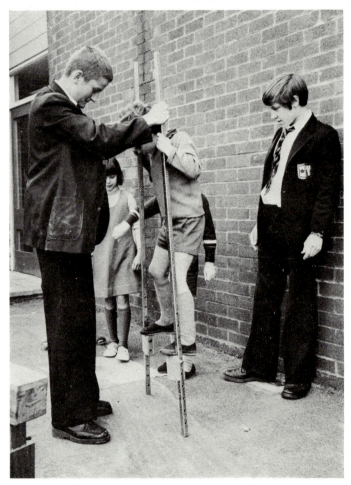

It was noticed during the observation period that very young children tended to stumble about in the playground during their PE lessons and at playtime. A number of boys devised various forms of play equipment designed to develop a sense of balance. These items ranged from various types of stilts, walking clogs, a skate-board, to a beam which adjusts in height and angle of inclination.

'I decided to make a play toy for the four to five-year-old nursery children that would be good fun but safe. I made a number of models first and measured the children so that the size was right. I have tested it with the children and it works very well. Now I am working on a packaging project and designing advertising material as if I were marketing the toy rocking boat for a firm.'

*'I thought the children would like to play in a model spaceship because the boys talk a lot about space flight. I am now forming a plastic dome for the top and then I am going to paint a lunar landscape on its sides.'*

*'The emphasis is on activity rather than just sitting.'*

The interest of young children in animals prompted designs for animal environments to replace the traditional cages in which rodents such as mice, gerbils and hamsters were kept. One pupil designed a biological experiment in which he hoped older children from St Mary's would make observations of how long it takes a mouse to learn its way around a maze to get to a food source.

Not all of the projects concerned the design and production of artefacts; some considered the child's environment within the school. A number of girls were engaged in making a mock-up of a 'soft' area made wholly of cushions and foam-filled shapes where children could recline or lounge, because they discovered that young children got tired during their active school day and needed periods of rest. A boy set about making road signs and painted arrows on the roadway leading to the school playground so that approaching traffic would not create a source of danger to the children. Although most pupils chose to work on individual projects, some formed themselves into groups, in some cases to tackle larger items. For instance, a boy and a group of girls decided to involve themselves in a fantasy theme about shops – the boy made a pet shop and the girls made animals out of fabric to stock it. Another group idea was to make a child-sized cage so that the children could play at being zoo animals, dressed in suitable play-sack costumes.

Most of the items designed required a number of visits between schools for our pupil designers to contact their lower-school clients, since they needed to discuss ideas, take personal measurements, show models and test prototypes. As pupils settled into the design realisation stage the number of visits became less frequent, but most pupils needed to return during production to check features of their designs.

However well conceived an idea is in the eyes of teachers and however much effort is involved in structuring a project, its success or failure depends not only on our ability as teachers to fire students' imaginations, but how it is received by them. The project described was generally well received. Few children were unable to develop ideas from situations they had observed and then convert them into design briefs. At the time of writing the project has still one term and a half to run, but enough has been produced to enable one to see the realised potential of this theme. The aim of presenting a more comprehensive designer/client situation has been largely achieved, and it would appear that this has helped in the development of attitudes in both upper and lower-school children by regular contacts throughout the period of this project. A by-product of the situation has been the depth of understanding gained by colleagues from the two schools of one another's objectives. Although our age ranges and methods are very different, our educational goals are in harmony.

Something of this relationship underlies two brief concluding comments about the project by the Headmaster and Deputy Headmistress of St Mary's Lower School:
'We have formed valuable links both with the staff and the pupils of Manshead School through this shared project. Besides the benefits of custom-designed play and learning equipment, our children have delighted in their contact with the older children in being interviewed, measured, asked to test items, and in visiting the studios and workshops of the upper school to see the various stages of production. Any fears we had of being disrupted or overwhelmed were unnecessary due to careful planning and preparation and also to the motivation sustained by the upper-school designers.'
Mrs M Shurmer
'Too often the only time teenagers are mentioned in the press or on the television is when they are involved in acts of vandalism or when they get into other forms of trouble. This is a totally unbalanced picture. Our experience through this project has shown how adolescents can demonstrate a real concern for others, as well as the obvious satisfaction gained through their creative experience.'
G H Clarke (Headmaster)

*Phil Mason is Head of the Design Faculty at Manshead School, Dunstable, an upper 13 to 18 comprehensive. The purpose-built accommodation for practical and design activities was new in 1971 and has a self-contained suite of workshops and studios.*

*The CSE Mode III course 'Combined Craft and Design' links the different facets of practical activity and has developed as the central core of the creative work. Not all work is integrated within the Design Faculty as a need for depth of experience as well as breadth is seen. Also there is a concern to develop work in conjunction with science and the humanities. Problem solving, the quality of individual expressions, consideration of the needs and feelings of others and the wider impact of design in the community are ideals upon which much of the work of the faculty has developed. Phil Mason is a founder member of the Bedfordshire Design Education Forum and is a present Treasurer of the National Association for Design Education.*

# Queen Elizabeth's School
## Stephen Burroughs

*Stephen Burroughs*

'Design education demands a way of thinking and a mode of action that tries to reconcile man to his environment by means of appropriate material solutions.

'In the first instance a deep understanding of human needs and problems is just as essential as the requirement for visual sensitivity towards form and structure. Perhaps in our hesitancy to make value judgements about the visual impact of artefacts we are afraid to applaud good form and proportion when we see it. Nature offers the perfect answer to many design problems and the relationship between form and function should not be forgotten. For example, it is no accident that the dorsal view of a trout corresponds to the cross-section of a modern aircraft wing. Today civil engineers, boatbuilders and aircraft designers all need to take full account of the necessary calculations for fluid dynamics. In a technological age when manufacturing and engineering account for more than half our exports, it is clear that our national survival is largely dependent on the production of well designed goods of high quality. Not all our children will become professional designers, but they will all be consumers. We should never try to legislate for "good taste", but education through the use of materials can help people to discriminate against shoddy goods and low environmental standards. Design education should not only be regarded as a bridge between science and humanities, it is a major component in a balanced school curriculum.'

The two examples chosen for this survey were major projects submitted as course work for the Oxford Board's A83 Design examination. These projects typify problems that affect individuals or groups of individuals within the community. Although they both depend on the use of the design process for a structured approach to problem solving, it can be seen that each project is very different in character. It is interesting to note the way in which some sections of the commonly used linear design process are emphasised or by-passed, and the sequence of operations changed.

### Fly Killers

Robin Wardle had looked at several possibilities for major projects, including a telescope stand for a rifle range and camp cooking equipment. However, these were either too specialised to be of general interest, or had been the subject of improved design in recent years.

Perhaps it was the mild winter and the warm summer that had helped to produce an unusually large number of flies of all species, including the house fly. The nuisance problem of flies in food preparation areas at school prompted an investigation into their significance in the spread of disease and possible methods of control and extermination. Eventually Robin decided to look into the possibility of producing some form of non-toxic fly killer.

Getting rid of flies is not a new problem, but it is only in this century that biologists have understood the major role of insects in the spread of common diseases. While looking at an article on Poster Graphics in a back copy of *Design* magazine, Robin noticed the excellent Health Education Council poster describing the repulsive feeding habits of the house fly. Clearly, the Health Education Council considered that the general public needed to be better informed about pests and diseases. It was decided that the whole area of fly killers was due for re-appraisal.

The stated problem was 'to control disease-carrying flies in the home without producing harmful side effects on humans, wild animals and pets'.

It must be appreciated that the study of the problem itself is as important as the study of the solutions. In this example, even the initial statement of the problem changed as a result of further investigation some weeks after the analysis had begun. Originally the stated problem or need was 'to kill disease-carrying flies', but it was seen that a more detailed specification was required. A whole host of other problems emerged when considering the use of toxic fly killers in kitchens, dining areas and children's rooms. In discussion around the school, some younger pupils reported that their goldfish had died after fly sprays had been used in the same room. It became apparent that the problem of fly killers was just part of the whole subject of pest control.

Robin was not a biologist, but he realised that a basic understanding of the life-cycle and feeding habits of the common house fly was essential for understanding methods of control. Reference books gave information about *Musca domestica* and the social implications resulting from the spread of typhoid, cholera, dysentry and tuberculosis. Manufacturers of chemical sprays and vaporisers gave literature and helpful information on pest control. The local authority's Public Health Officer outlined his responsibilities and gave the student some publicity material. The Consumers' Association magazine *Which?* had surveyed all domestic chemical insecticides in July 1969.

All this data was kept as written reference material in a major project folder. It would have been unwise to ignore existing solutions and essential data for a problem that had been with us for so long.

Possible methods of control consisted of pressurised chemical sprays, hot thermal vaporisers, slow release strips, sticky fly-papers, fly swatters, ultra-violet light and perhaps fly eating plants.

In the *Which?* report on insecticides, it was found that many sprays were good at killing flies, but some contained DDT and Lindane, both persistent chemicals and a danger to the environment. Only pyrethrum was considered to be reasonably safe. Fluoro-carbons were used as propellant gases in aerosols; their effect on the break-up of the ozone layer is still debated by scientists.

All the information obtained seemed to point to a need for a conservationist approach to the problem, and so Robin decided to exclude the use of chemicals. Even ultra-violet light attractants, as used in fish shops and butchers, were discounted because long term exposure to humans could result in skin cancer, in addition to their continuous consumption of electricity.

It became apparent that a completely original solution to the problem was unlikely. At one stage, Robin thought that there was little he could do to make a serious design contribution and felt like giving up. However, he was worried that most people were buying chemical fly killers and using them in places not recommended by the manufacturers. All too often the toxic, slow-release vapour strips marketed by the large chemical companies could be seen hanging in kitchens, childrens' rooms, bakeries and food preparation areas. It is well known that bread, for example, is easily tainted by organic chemicals. (Sandwiches left for a short while in a room next to the school project area had become quite unpalatable after absorbing the styrene vapour produced while building glass fibre canoes.) While there was no direct clinical evidence to cause alarm, there was enough circumstantial evidence to indicate that the long-term effects of exposure to toxic fly killers might be harmful. For this reason Robin restricted his attention to the two 'safe' methods of fly control – fly swatters and sticky fly-paper.

A really efficient fly swatter was required, and possibly something more attractive than a sticky fly paper morgue hanging from the light bulb. These preliminary ideas were developed on a series of sketch sheets for discussion between teacher and student.

It was found that rolled newspapers and towels used to kill flies often set up warning air currents. The optimum shapes for a fly swatter were those with an aerofoil section for the stem and blade. However, since several angles of attack might be employed, a compromise was made and round or oval cross-sections were used. The ideal shape, size and weight of the fly swatter was discovered by making sketches and prototypes. It was to be a natural extension of the hand. The handle itself had to fulfil the best ergonomic function, and several shapes were developed. The 'grid' was designed to stun rather than crush completely. It was soon discovered that some skill in tactics was needed – flies take off backwards!

Materials such as cane, wood, leather and plastics were considered. Nylon for the stem and polyethylene for the blade were used on the final product. There were problems in joining wood, metal, nylon and polythene together. Injection moulding was suggested for commercial production, although the school did not have the facilities for this.

Common reactions to the candidate using the prototype in school were interesting. When questioned about this, Robin said 'They seem to think I'm some kind of sadist! People don't realise that their health is at stake.' The critics were soon very anxious to have a go themselves!

The traditional fly-paper is still obtainable from ironmongers, and sales have increased, especially with pet owners, perhaps as a result of environmentalist pressure. However,

*'Flies can take off backwards!'*

*Right: ideas for mobiles and traps by 13-year-old foundation students.*

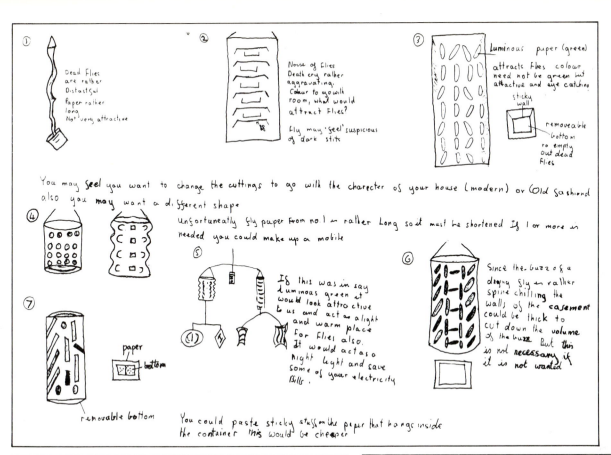

1. Dead Flies are rather Distastful Paper rather long Not very attractive

2. Noise of Flies Death cry rather aggravating. Colour to go with room, what would attract Flies?

Fly may 'feel' suspicious of dark slits

3. luminous paper (green) attracts Flies colour need not be green but attractive and eye catching

sticky wall

removeable bottom to empty out dead Flies

You may feel you want to change the cuttings to go with the character of your house (modern) or (Old fashiond also you may want a different shape

4.

Unfortuneatly fly paper from no 1 is rather Long so it must be shortened If 1 or more is needed you could make up a mobile

5. If this was in say luminous green it would look attractive to us and act as a light and warm place for Flies also. It would act as a night light and save some of your electricity bills.

6. Since the buzz of a dieing fly is rather spine chilling the walls of the casement could be thick to cut down the volume of the buzz But this is not necessary if it is not wanted

7.

paper

bottom

removable bottom

You could paste sticky stuff on the paper that hangs inside the container this would be cheaper

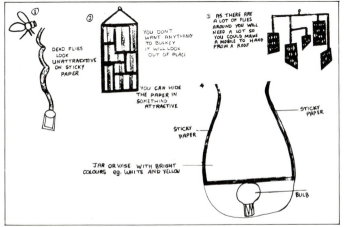

1. DEAD FLIES LOOK UNATTRACTIVE ON STICKY PAPER

2. YOU DON'T WANT ANYTHING TO BULKEY IT WILL LOOK OUT OF PLACE

YOU CAN HIDE THE PAPER IN SOMETHING ATTRACTIVE

3. AS THERE ARE A LOT OF FLIES AROUND YOU WILL NEED A LOT SO YOU COULD MAKE A MOBILE TO HANG FROM A ROOF

4. STICKY PAPER

STICKY PAPER

JAR OR VASE WITH BRIGHT COLOURS eg. WHITE AND YELLOW

BULB

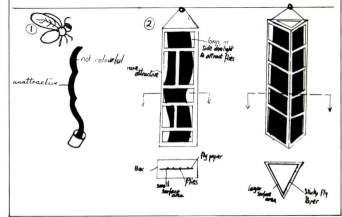

1. not colourful

unattractive

2. lamp in side give light to attract flies

more attractive

Box

fly paper

Flies

small surface area

larger surface area

Sticky fly paper

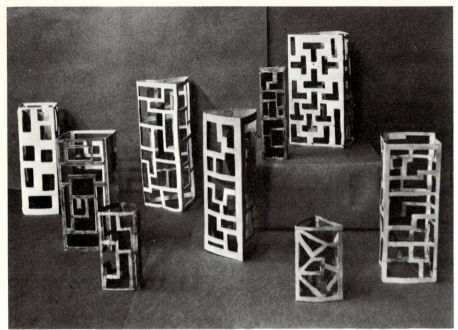

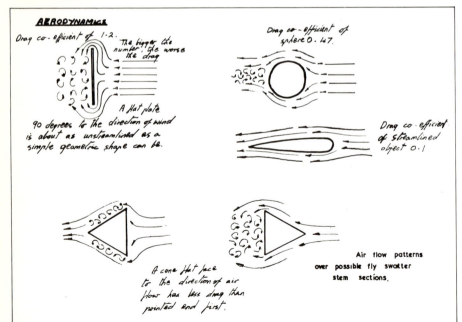

Above left: 'The completed mobiles have strong patterns to camouflage the sticky fly-paper.'

Above: traditional fly-paper and a louvred mobile with disposable paper.

Left: details showing air flow around the stem and head of the fly swatter.

Above right: the completed fly swatter with alternative heads.

many people have a natural revulsion to fly-papers hanging above the dining table. Robin wanted to design a 'mask' or camouflage to disguise the obvious function of the trap. Basic concepts of space and pattern were explored in card 'lanterns' for mobiles. This problem was given to a group of 13-year-old girls who produced some useful ideas. In discussion with a British manufacturer of fly-papers it was suggested that flies attract more flies. On observation it was noticeable that the number of flies caught increased rapidly after the first half dozen or so had been trapped. Perhaps 'a crowd draws a crowd', even in the insect world. One answer was to print fly shapes on the sticky paper. A university zoology research department was also discovered to be trying to isolate the sex hormone to act as an attractant, although this was not possible in commercial quantities.

In order to disguise the sticky fly-paper, a variety of partially enclosing structures was developed. A quantity of fly-gum and paper was kindly donated by a manufacturer. (The gum is principally a mixture of masticated rubber, anti-drying agents and colour and contains no harmful chemicals.) Prototype fly traps were made with disposable sticky cards. A variety of shapes for mobiles and fluorescent and pendant light fittings

were also designed. Materials such as paper, balsa wood, wire and card were mainly used.

The fly swatter was generally a successful end product, although not significantly better than a commercially imported type. The candidate learnt a great deal, however, about the physical properties of plastics and methods of working and joining.

A 'consumer test' revealed that some skill was required to achieve a consistent success rate. Sixth-form badminton and tennis players were the most effective users! There were obvious disadvantages for young children or the infirm. Other tests indicated that the fly swatter was the only effective way of killing invading wasps and large flies.

The sticky fly traps were not so successful. When talking to Robin about this he admitted that there was much more research to be done. 'Flies seem to "prefer" the traditional sticky paper', he said. There were also weaknesses in the testing procedure. Some prototype fly traps were tested in the winter months and attempts to hatch fly larvae (angler's maggots) produced only hordes of *Calliphora erythrocephala*, the large bluebottle. These crawled over the sticky fly-paper quite happily and had to be killed with the swatter.

In spite of this, Robin felt that the project had given him a tremendous insight into the problem of a safe but effective control system. 'The general public are so ignorant about preventive measures that should be taken, it should all begin in the schools', he suggested.

When questioned about the A-level course, Robin thought that the discipline of the design process was of immense personal assistance when tackling all kinds of problems outside design work itself. It helped him to organise his thinking for a whole range of tasks, from rebuilding a motorcycle engine to answering questions at interviews. He thought that more people could benefit from this form of education.

## Playgroup furniture

The playgroup furniture project arose out of a need for cheap play equipment and furniture for pre-school playgroups in the district. Nureen Sadeghi had spent some time thinking about topics for a major project and decided that she was particularly interested in the social and human factors affecting design work. She was also interested in young children and had easy access to one of the local playgroups.

The problem was to provide inexpensive seating, work surfaces and play equipment for pre-school children.

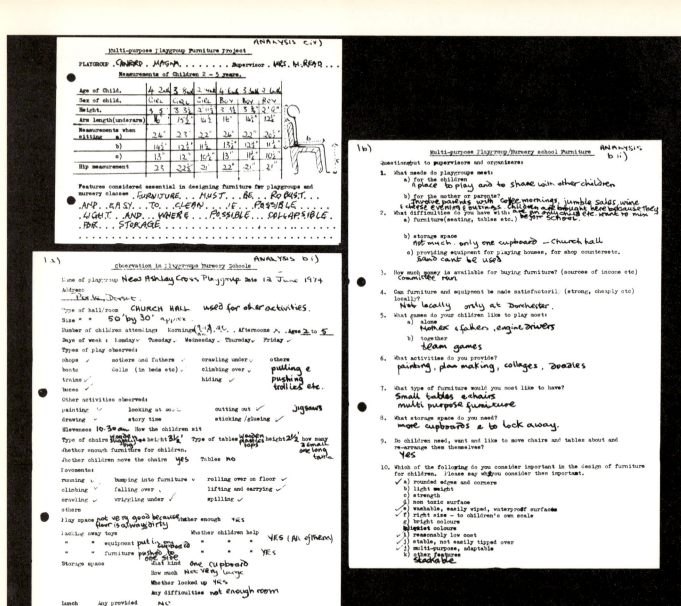

**Multi-purpose Playgroup Furniture Project**

PLAYGROUP . CANFORD . MAGNA . . . . . . . Supervisor . MRS. M. READ . . .

**Measurements of Children 2 – 5 years.**

| Age of Child. | 4 2mth | 3 8mth | 2 4mth | 4 6mth | 3 3mth | 2 6mth |
|---|---|---|---|---|---|---|
| Sex of child. | GIRL | GIRL | GIRL | BOY | BOY | BOY |
| Height. | 3'5" | 3'3½" | 2'11½" | 3'3½" | 3'3¾" | 2'6" |
| Arm length (underarm) | 16 | 15½" | 14½" | 16" | 14½" | 12½" |
| Measurements when sitting a) | 24" | 23" | 22" | 24" | 22" | 20½" |
| b) | 14½" | 12½" | 11½" | 13½" | 12½" | 11½" |
| c) | 13" | 12" | 10½" | 13" | 11½" | 10½" |
| Hip measurement | 23 | 22½ | 21 | 22" | 21" | 21" |

Features considered essential in designing furniture for playgroups and nursery classes . FURNITURE . . MUST . . BE . . ROBUST . . AND . EASY . TO . CLEAN . IF . POSSIBLE . . . . . LIGHT . AND . WHERE . . POSSIBLE . . COLLAPSIBLE . . FOR . . STORAGE . . . . . . . . . . . . . . . . .

---

1 a)

**Observation in Playgroups Nursery Schools**   ANALYSIS b i)

Name of playgroup New Ashley Cross Playgroup Date 12 June 1974
Address Poole, Dorset.
Type of hall/room CHURCH HALL used for other activities.
Size " 50' by 30' approx.
Number of children attending: Morning 9-12 a.c. Afternoons × Ages 2 to 5
Days of week : Monday. Tuesday. Wednesday. Thursday. Friday.
Types of play observed:

shops ✓  mothers and fathers ✓  crawling under ✓  others
boats  dolls (in beds etc) ✓  climbing over ✓  pulling &
trains ✓  hiding ✓  pushing
buses ✓  trolleys etc.

Other activities observed:
painting ✓  looking at books  cutting out ✓  jigsaws
drawing ✓  story time  sticking /glueing ✓

Elevenses 10.30 am How the children sit
Type of chairs wooden too big height 8½" Type of tables wooden plastic tops height 2½' how many 2 small one long table
Whether enough furniture to sit
Whether children move the chairs YES Tables NO
Movements:

running ✓  bumping into furniture ✓  rolling over on floor ✓
climbing ✓  falling over ✓  lifting and carrying ✓
crawling ✓  wriggling under ✓  spilling ✓

others
Play space not very good because floor is always dirty  Whether enough YES
Packing away toys  Whether children help YES (All of them)
" equipment put in one cupboard " " " YES (All of them)
" furniture pushed to one side " " " YES
Storage space What kind one cupboard
How much Not very large
Whether locked up YES
Any difficulties not enough room
Lunch Any provided NO
Seating and tables
Any special needs. Better furniture.

General observations (scaling, variations in sizes of children – abilities etc. group or individual play.....)
More furniture is needed which is to scale with the children
Not a very large difference in the children's sizes

---

1 b)

**Multi-purpose Playgroup/Nursery school Furniture**   ANALYSIS b ii)

Questions put to supervisors and organizers:

1. What needs do playgroups meet:
   a) for the children
      A place to play and to share with other children
   b) for the mother or parents?
      Involve parents with coffee mornings, jumble sales, wine & cheese evenings & outings. Children are brought here because they are an only child etc. want to mix before school.
2. What difficulties do you have with:
   a) furniture (seating, tables etc.)
   b) storage space
      Not much. only one cupboard – church hall
   c) providing equipment for playing houses, for shop counters etc.
      Sand cant be used
3. How much money is available for buying furniture? (sources of income etc)
   Committee run
4. Can furniture and equipment be made satisfactorily (strong, cheaply etc) locally?
   Not locally only at Dorchester.
5. What games do your children like to play most:
   a) alone
      Mother & fathers, engine drivers
   b) together
      team games
6. What activities do you provide?
   painting, plan making, collages, doodles
7. What type of furniture would you most like to have?
   Small tables & chairs multi purpose furniture
8. What storage space do you need?
   more cupboards & to lock away.
9. Do children need, want and like to move chairs and tables about and re-arrange them themselves?
   YES
10. Which of the following do you consider important in the design of furniture for children. Please say why you consider them important.
   ✓ a) rounded edges and corners
   b) light weight
   c) strength
   d) non toxic surface
   ✓ e) washable, easily wiped, waterproof surfaces
   ✓ f) right size – to children's own scale
   g) bright colours
   h) quiet colours
   ✓ i) reasonably low cost
   ✓ j) stable, not easily tipped over
   ✓ j) multi-purpose, adaptable
   k) other features
      Stackable

The analysis stage required data collection and research for the whole area of the problem and involved an understanding of child psychology and the importance of play. Preliminary reading demanded references to Froebel, Piaget and Bloom for concepts of child development. Froebel said 'Play is the highest expression of human development in childhood'. Piaget saw play as part of the child's response to the environment. He saw the need to provide the right type of environment and situation at each stage of development so that a child's potential could be fully realised. It was discovered that most theories of play pointed to the fact that play is not an end in itself, but that it has an educational function in preparing children for a full adult role in later life.

'Play is generally believed to be one of the principal ways in which a child learns how to give as well as take, and in so doing he learns how to adapt to adult society as he grows up. Between birth and maturity, the child comes to terms with the world around him, and comes to accept that he has to take his fellows into account. The extent to which a child successfully learns how to live in and not outside society depends on a wide range of factors. These include not only his genetic inheritance, the social and physical background of his family, educational facilities and relationships with parents, but also the opportunity for play.' (*Children at Play*, Department of the Environment, HMSO 1973.)

Nureen visited playgroups and nursery schools, observing children and listening to what they said. She found that many children, especially girls, disliked the sophisticated constructional toys approved by some educationists. These were especially irrelevant when acting out parent roles of playing shops, hospitals or dressing up. There were also other activities such as painting and modelling that required other kinds of equipment. In general, the simplest improvised materials led to really imaginative play.

It became apparent that Nureen had to satisfy the very diverse requirements of seating, storage, tables and toys. Anthropometric and ergonomic data for this age range were well documented and easily obtained.

Existing solutions, such as miniature adult chairs and tables, were rejected because their shape and form did not allow for the play and storage requirements of the design brief. 'In any case', said Nureen, 'we should not try to impose adult constraints on children at this age. Since the greatest emphasis at play school is on activity rather than sitting, the children don't need expensive chairs and tables.'

This candidate's two-dimensional work was slightly limited by a lack of previous full art room experience and this tended to affect her fluency in producing sketch sheets of preliminary ideas. 'I know what it should look like but it is not easy to draw', is a common cry from students starting design in the sixth form for the first time. Nevertheless, Nureen produced an excellent folder of work sheets, and eventually three-dimensional ideas were quickly formulated using card, expanded polystyrene and Perspex. A modular system of cube units was soon developed. These could be used as receptacles or containers for storage and surfaces on which to sit or write. At this stage it was suggested by the tutor that there was a need to explore other possibilities for stacking and linking modular units of different shapes, using common geometrical solids. These ideas for promoting divergent thinking were developed, but not adopted because they could not fulfil all the storage functions. Nureen knew what was wanted and she was able to justify it in terms of the original brief.

It was discovered that there were far more imaginative possibilities for play if simple open box units were chosen. These consisted of three-sided units with back and sides joining at right angles giving the basis of the whole range of equipment. Supports at different levels in the units enabled the seat and shelf boards to be moved into different positions for tables, chairs, shelf units, cupboards, beds, climbing apparatus and many other necessary pieces of equipment.

Scaling to suit the fast-growing two to five age group necessitated the measurement of children at various playgroups, and the recording of information about activities, storage, refreshments and facilities by questionnaire.

After looking at plastics, and at natural and manufactured wooden boards, Nureen thought that plywood would be the most appropriate material for the units. Although she had little previous workshop experience, she felt able to undertake a project in wood. One of the first structural design problems was how to overcome the inherent weakness of an open three-sided unit, keeping the corners at right angles and maintaining rigidity. This issue was not fully resolved until the final stages. It was decided to use two laminated ash support rails in each unit, both for seat support and rigidity. The idea was a good one, but in practice there were difficulties in steam bending, drying and glueing. A special jig was made to give dimensional accuracy, but it was not possible to get consistent pressure with G-cramps, and the laminated hoop failed when tested. Resorcinol formaldehyde glue would have given a better bond,

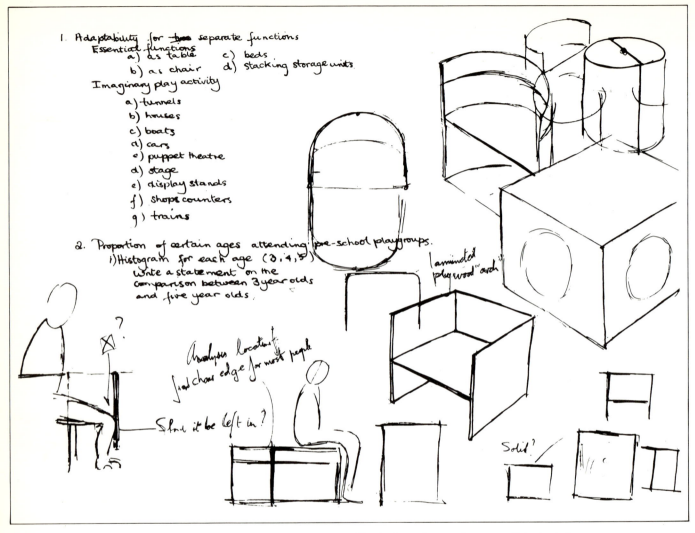

1. Adaptability for two separate functions
   Essential functions
       a) as table   c) beds
       b) as chair   d) stacking storage units
   Imaginary play activity
       a) tunnels
       b) houses
       c) boats
       d) cars
       e) puppet theatre
       d) stage
       e) display stands
       f) shop counters
       g) trains

2. Proportion of certain ages attending pre-school playgroups.
   i) Histogram for each age (3,4,5)
   write a statement on the
   comparison between 3 year olds
   and five year olds.

?

Analysis location?
find chair edge for most people

Should it be left in?

laminated
plywood "arch"

Solid?

*Sketch sheets from early stages of the project.*

and a pneumatic tube would have provided the even pressure required. An alternative system using battens strengthened with steel corner plates was chosen. Before deciding on the support rail system, many ideas were explored for fixing the seat boards into position including slots and grooves, and a variety of pegs, dowels and other patent fastenings.

The initial joining of the plywood sides and back at the corners presented an interesting problem. Traditional joints were not considered appropriate for the material being used, or for quantity production. Instead, knock-down fittings of the barrel nut and socket cap screw type were chosen. This enabled the whole assembly to be joined by using a hexagonal

a) Function as a table

i) Surface area – is it adequate for one child?. is it adequate for two children? No
(One table unit for one child)

ii) rigidity
↓
construction?
   – limitations and constraints
      1) inevitably turned over to make a chair ∴ simple shape and form required to give max. adaptability.

iii) most tables have legs! Why? – allows a rigid leg and rail construction of great economy to be used.

iv) slab sides for supports pose new construction problems.

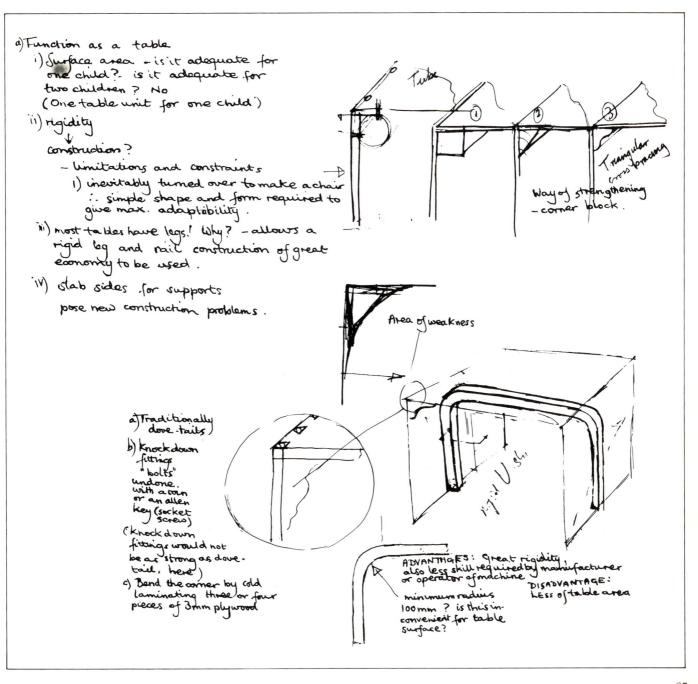

Tube

① ② ③

Triangular cross bracing

Way of strengthening – corner block.

Area of weakness

a) Traditionally dove-tails)

b) Knock down fittings "bolts" undone. with a coin or an allen key (socket screw)

(knock down fittings would not be as strong as dove-tail, here)

c) Bend the corner by cold laminating three or four pieces of 3mm plywood

minimum radius 100mm? is this inconvenient for table surface?

ADVANTAGES: Great rigidity also less skill required by manufacturer or operator of machine

DISADVANTAGE: Less of table area

key. The 'flat-pack' furniture could be produced and transported more cheaply, leaving the final assembly to be completed at the playgroup.

Another problem was preventing the units slipping when in the stacked position. This was resolved by experimenting with various interlocking shapes in Perspex. A number of different angles and projections were tried. Finally, a shallow projection on each top edge with a taper of 3° was used, giving stability and yet easy removal.

Foam cushions were made up for the seat backs and bed, and four complete multi-purpose play units were produced for final assessment.

The multi-purpose units were extremely well received by the children and the playgroup leaders. When introducing the units to the first playgroup it was thought that some guidance or encouragement might be necessary before the children would use them naturally. In fact, after setting up the basic units the children began to take over completely, and were full of ideas that had not been considered during the design stage. It was discovered that the box units could be grouped to provide a whole range of props for play activities, including ships, buses, trains, cars, shops, bridges and climbing apparatus.

Although the units were not tested to destruction or left in a play school for more than a short period, it was clear that they had been an instant success. Some minor modifications of size and shape would be necessary before commercial production could be considered. There is no doubt that this design could become a viable proposition if adopted by a manufacturer.

Nureen found the practical work a major undertaking and would have benefitted from some experience in working with materials earlier in her school career. Nevertheless she enjoyed the practical work and was rewarded with a tremendous sense of personal success in a new subject area.

'I am glad I did A-level Design, it's so different from other school subjects – very demanding, but directly relevant to life.'

To summarise, it must be stated that the two selected examples were not chosen because the candidates received good grades, but rather because they illustrate the wide variety of course work that can be offered for assessment.

In both examples the functional requirements were analysed as objectively as possible. The fly killer problem demanded technical and scientific research with controlled experiments over a long period. These experiments were not fully completed during the investigation phase of the project.

*Scale models of play units.*

*Right: the units had to be portable;*
*units stacked to provide shelving and storage space;*
*two units converted for use as a bed.*

Because of this, the candidate decided to opt for workable solutions that he could undertake more easily. The fly traps called for a strong visual camouflage with an attractive pattern and form. Here, the more expressive factors such as space and structure were of prime importance. Further ideas for hanging mobiles could have been more fully developed. The fly swatter was more successful and could easily be modified for quantity production.

In all, the non-toxic fly killer project should be regarded as a courageous attempt to tackle a problem that should be examined more closely by commercial manufacturers.

The design analysis for playgroup furniture involved an investigation into the needs of young children. This was an area with which the candidate was reasonably familiar. She was able to observe activity, record verbal reactions and take physical measurements. Her research was very thorough and although this in itself did not provide the ideas, it prevented

any obvious mistakes being made. In this example, human requirements were clearly recognised and largely dictated the final form of the end product. Although a high level of technical skill was not required, a considerable amount of time was required for the construction of the units. This was necessary since a minimum of four units was needed for the evaluation of group activity. Both candidates required the resources of technology, but functional needs are inextricably bound up with human needs. Frequently these interacting elements result in an agreeable compromise solution. Critics may say that the sequential design process does not allow for the development of individual excellence. It is important to ensure that the course is not so tightly structured that it inhibits the flair and divergent thinking of gifted students. On this course a team teaching approach was used, and although largely directed by one member of staff, both students were able to discuss ideas with other specialist staff in the school. The continuous assessment method allowed candidates to progress

naturally through all the design stages, consulting outside establishments and obtaining help from local government authorities and industry. In these 'real-life' experiences it was possible to make judgements that could be artificial under a closed examination system.

Both students seemed to learn as much about people as they did about materials, and they developed a maturity towards social design problems. Of course, the best work cannot be done without adequate facilities, but even in design education, teachers and children are still the main resources.

*Stephen Burroughs is Head of the Design and Technology Department at Queen Elizabeth's School and introduced the A-level Design course in order to co-ordinate the various subject disciplines within the department. Design work is seen as an integral part of the whole school curriculum but with special links with both art and applied science. At the same time he feels design teaching possesses an ethos in its own right, based on the*

analysis and solution of real-life problems. Queen Elizabeth's is an upper school of 1450 pupils in a three tier comprehensive system. Thirteen-year-old pupils coming from three middle schools will have received a broad sampling experience in art, home economics, metalwork, needlework and woodwork prior to opting for three of these areas in the upper school. During the foundation year at the upper school, pupils in the design and technology area are introduced to basic problem analysis and an understanding of the physical and visual characteristics of wood, metal and plastics. Communication skills (technical drawing and graphics) and workshop skills are developed during assignments. In addition, written projects on the work of famous architects, engineers and designers are undertaken during the year.

In the fourth year, pupils may opt for either the traditional subject disciplines such as art, engineering, metalwork, technical drawing and woodwork, or take the combined design courses to CSE or O-level. Those who have not taken creative subjects to examination level in the fifth year are not excluded from the A-level design course, but those offering craft and design with art or physics are at a distinct advantage. Pupils are advised that careers in architecture, civil and mechanical engineering, industrial design and town planning are open to those taking design with an appropriate combination of other A-levels.

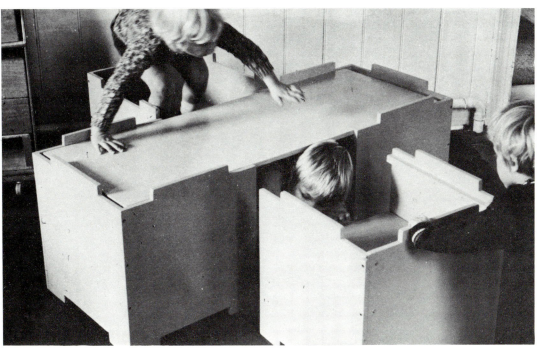

# Pimlico School

## Eileen Adams

*Eileen Adams*

*'I regard education as being concerned with relationships and communication with pupils, colleagues and sources outside the school. I am also interested in the interrelationship of areas of experience and knowledge, and how we communicate ideas. I find the examination-dominated curriculum concerned with objective academic study promoted through subject disciplines inadequate for meeting the needs of too many pupils. The teaching of both art and design has also been dominated by ideas more relevant to post-school experience and professional training and not necessarily applicable to children in school. We are still concerned with what children can remember, or know about or produce, rather than what they feel, how they understand and what they experience. As teachers of art and design I feel we have been concerned more with 'products' than with extending sensibility, though art is one of the few subjects that values a subjective, affective response.*

*'The contribution that can be made by art teachers in the context of aesthetic, design or environmental education is considerable, if they choose to recognise their responsibilities. Just as we have to learn to speak or to read, we need to be taught to "see", to become perceptive, to have confidence in our judgements and be responsible for our decisions.'*

For the past few years my particular concern as an art teacher has been with the interrelation of the child and environment – the child's experience, understanding and attempts to make sense of it, particularly through visual study, and the environment as a learning resource, stimulus and field of study. Teaching in London schools, my concern has been mainly with the urban, man-made environment.

From 1974 to 1976, I was involved in Front Door, an experimental project at Pimlico School that was an attempt to devise a course of architectural and design studies based on an investigation of the local area. The project team comprised art teachers from the school, architects from the Greater London Council and Ken Baynes from the Royal College of Art 'Design in Education' research team. We also referred to other outside sources of information and support when necessary for the development of the study.

The first aim of the project was to devise forms of architectural education that were based on the pupils' own direct experience of the environment. The second was to assess the possible role of local authority architects in the improvement of general architectural education. The third, finally, was to assess the specific contribution that art departments could make to general architectural education. Overall we aimed to develop a long-term coherent course of architectural and design studies as part of everyone's environmental education, rather than limit the scope of the project to a particular age range or option group. Based in the art department, the work had a strong visual bias.

The problem we set ourselves was to find the best ways of promoting direct study approaches for the different ages and abilities of pupils in a large inner-city comprehensive school of 1650 pupils: how to collect information, how to interpret and evaluate it and how to communicate ideas.

Front Door was introduced as a compulsory course for the lower school and as an option for the fourth-year pupils. The first and second years followed a Front Door course for three periods a week for a term, spending the other two terms in the home economics and design and technology departments. Each department contributed in some measure to environmental education – home economics dealing with the domestic environment of the home; design and technology dealing with the technical environment of tools and artefacts; and Front Door dealing with the urban environment.

Design education, as the first and second years were encouraged to understand it, was an exploration of how man shapes and controls his environment. The course was experimental, and co-operation between departments involved was still in the early stages of development. The pupils saw it as reasonable and valid that they make a study of the urban environment primarily through a visual approach, as they had been used to practical study in other areas. They did not seem to be inhibited about drawing because a lot of them found it easier than reading and writing.

The first-years studied the concept of 'neighbourhood', which involved local trails, streetwork, museum visits and follow-up work in the classroom. Everything was related to the

*First-year: journey to school.*

local environment or the child's own neighbourhood, and information and ideas were expressed through drawing, writing and painting. The favourite studies in the scheme were concerned with an investigation of the journey to school and a Pimlico trail. This necessitated a museum visit to check up on the background to the development of the area, a study of the child's own neighbourhood and home. The children explored their relationships with their environment by expressing their views and suggesting ideas for improvement, attempting a glimpse of future possibilities. All the work was on A2 sized paper so that the pupils built up their own scrapbooks.

The second-year scheme concentrated on the exploration and development of visual ideas such as shape, colour, pattern and texture. The work demanded close observation, careful visual analysis, and the development of ideas in a variety of media. Popular studies in this year were screen printed fabrics, based on a study of windows at a local council estate; a

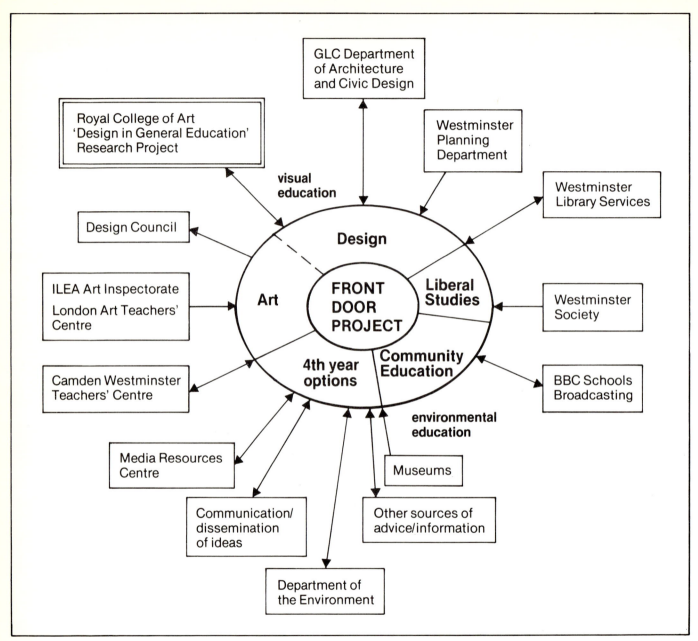

GLC Department of Architecture and Civic Design

Royal College of Art 'Design in General Education' Research Project

Westminster Planning Department

Westminster Library Services

**visual education**

Design Council

**Design**

Westminster Society

**Art**

**FRONT DOOR PROJECT**

**Liberal Studies**

ILEA Art Inspectorate London Art Teachers' Centre

Westminster Society

**Community Education**

Camden Westminster Teachers' Centre

**4th year options**

BBC Schools Broadcasting

**environmental education**

Media Resources Centre

Museums

Communication/ dissemination of ideas

Other sources of advice/information

Department of the Environment

*Involvement of outside agencies in the Front Door project.*

*Right: the planned pattern of Front Door courses at Pimlico in the first year of the project.*

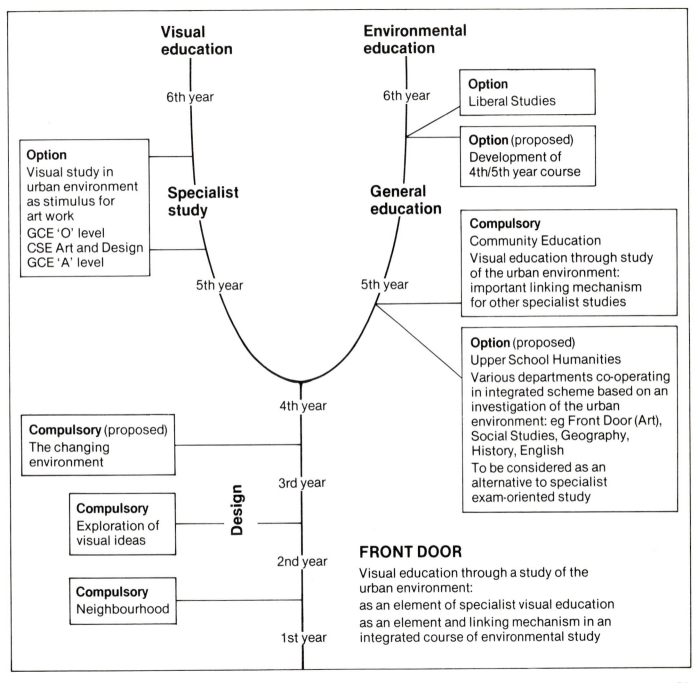

**Visual education**

6th year

**Option**
Visual study in urban environment as stimulus for art work
GCE 'O' level
CSE Art and Design
GCE 'A' level

**Specialist study**

5th year

4th year

**Compulsory** (proposed)
The changing environment

3rd year

**Design**

**Compulsory**
Exploration of visual ideas

2nd year

**Compulsory**
Neighbourhood

1st year

**Environmental education**

6th year

**Option**
Liberal Studies

**Option** (proposed)
Development of 4th/5th year course

**General education**

5th year

**Compulsory**
Community Education
Visual education through study of the urban environment: important linking mechanism for other specialist studies

**Option** (proposed)
Upper School Humanities
Various departments co-operating in integrated scheme based on an investigation of the urban environment: eg Front Door (Art), Social Studies, Geography, History, English
To be considered as an alternative to specialist exam-oriented study

**FRONT DOOR**

Visual education through a study of the urban environment:
as an element of specialist visual education
as an element and linking mechanism in an integrated course of environmental study

collection of coal hole cover cutouts; a ceramic panel, based on studies of the art room; large paper collages of pattern, based on repetition of shapes found in the swimming bath, balustrades, swings, railings, windows, paving stones, walls and car

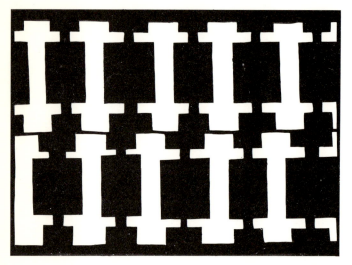

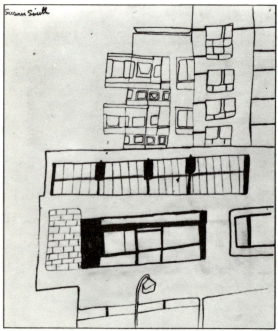

*Second-year: drawings and patterns based on repetition of shape.*

*Above and overleaf: fourth-year photographic studies.*

tyres. This took the children on an exciting trail in search of material. Excitement and interest were key features of these discovery trails – a search for a squirrel in Pimlico was really a study of Victorian decoration based on natural form, noting acorn topped railings, cast iron leafy plant holders and flower-shaped glass panels, ending up with the discovery of a squirrel as a balcony support. The ordinary everyday aspects of the environment took on a new importance, and the children were eager to report on their latest 'finds'. We all have different perceptions of our environment, and it was interesting to compare the reactions of the lower-school classes with those of the fourth year – the younger ones had an eye for detail or humour, while the older pupils displayed a growing social awareness.

The fourth-years opted to follow a Front Door course for two periods a week for a year instead of following the Community Education course. They were from different form groups, with different abilities and interests. Some had also chosen art as one of their options, while others were only too pleased to have given it up, not seeing it as a worthwhile or relevant subject for study.

Front Door groups were, therefore, made up of pupils interested in the environment or photography, or who had less interest in the alternative Community Education course.

This dictated certain methods of working, as many of the pupils did not have sufficient confidence to learn through the methods normally adopted by the art department at fourth-year level – for instance, many of the pupils had a block about drawing, but did not have the same inhibition about using a camera. Some of the pupils were interested in photography, but none of them knew much about it, which made us decide to make slide programmes initially, so that we could tackle problems of processing gradually, once we had become familiar with using a camera and establishing some basic confidence in handling the photographic medium.

The teachers involved did not have much photographic

experience either, so the support of the school's media resources officer and the warden of the art teachers' centre was enlisted. The MRO helped in the classroom, and the teachers' centre organised a number of two-day courses for pupils and teachers to learn basic camera usage and processing techniques. As well as providing a means for cheap in-service training, this reinforced the group feeling of everyone, as both pupils and teachers, being members of an investigatory team, learned through participation in a study that was relatively new to all.

The value of the short intensive course as an introduction to photography was that it gave more lesson time for active study, and in two days the pupils probably learned as much as they would normally have done in a term.

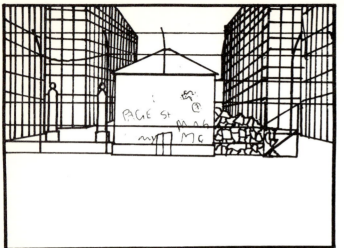

Programmes produced by the pupils covered housing, shops, transport, demolition and redevelopment, play provision and windows, words and street furniture. The work had a strong visual bias, but the pupils were also asked to provide a taped commentary. The choice of subjects could equally well have been made by a social studies group, for whom the programmes were prepared. The method of study and presentation of ideas could easily have been incorporated into the social studies syllabus, and it was hoped that an art teacher and social studies teacher would co-operate in developing such a syllabus the following year. The slide programmes were used as stimulus or reinforcement material for younger classes

*Fourth-year: play provision study*

*Above: Page Street 'playground' drawn and photographed.*

*Right: scheme for improvement.*

*Opposite: the playground's present layout and a scheme for improvement.*

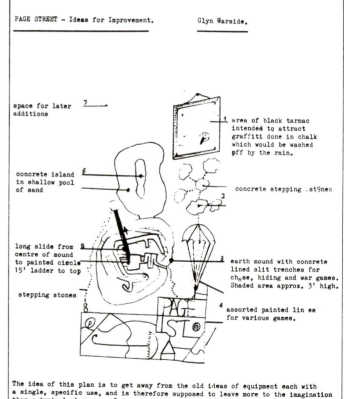

PAGE STREET – Ideas for Improvement.          Glyn Warside.

space for later additions — 7

concrete island in shallow pool of sand — 6

long slide from centre of mound to painted circle 15' ladder to top — 5

stepping stones — 1

1 — area of black tarmac intended to attract graffiti done in chalk which would be washed off by the rain.

concrete stepping stones — 2

3 — earth mound with concrete lined slit trenches for chase, hiding and war games. Shaded area approx. 3' high.

4 — assorted painted lines for various games.

The idea of this plan is to get away from the old ideas of equipment each with a single, specific use, and is therefore supposed to leave more to the imagination than a typical play area. I suspect however, that this is too structured, due to my being conditioned to expect structured play areas. Parts of it are improvised on items for play at Laycock Primary School.

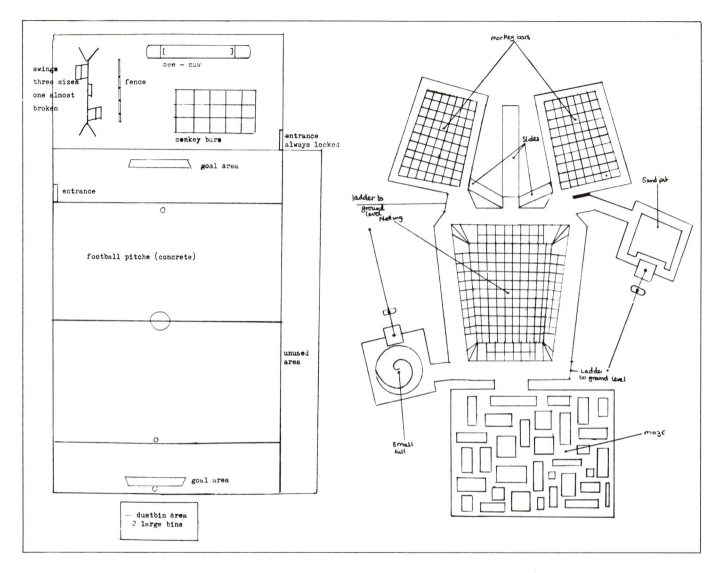

too, and fourth-years were invited to attend the lesson to see their programme in use, so that further adjustments could be made for improvement, depending on the audience reaction.

Through this activity we were involved in making two filmstrips with the BBC, and we were therefore able to share our work with other schools. The BBC Radiovision filmstrip 'Town Centres and Shopping Areas' in the Art and

Humanities series, looks at 'signals' transmitted to potential shoppers by the display of goods and design of shops, and contrasts the scale of traditional shops and shopping with supermarkets. The second filmstrip is included in a study box, 'Front Door – Broadcasting and the Architectural Environment', which is about the fourth-years working on their slide programmes. It is available on loan from the Schools Broadcasting Council.

Other fourth-year pupils in some of the art groups were also able to develop different studies in the local area through drawing and painting, which involved outdoor sketching sessions, this work being used for further development back in the art studio. This type of study was well suited to the CSE and GCE O-level courses in that it demanded visual discrimination and critical awareness in the selection of material; observation and analysis in the recording of information; and imagination and sensitivity in the development of ideas.

I do not believe there is any one school subject that can cope adequately with the complex and comprehensive nature of environmental education, though many subjects can involve themselves in environmental study. If we consider our attempt to educate children about the environment through the medium of our specialist discipline, we realise that there are a number of possible approaches, each aimed at making sense of the environment.

The environment can be perceived, studied directly and comprehended in a number of ways. First as a static reality, which may relate well to art studies, for example a shape, a colour, a heap of stone or a cat on a fence. Second, it may be understood as a dynamic reality, a series of working systems, more appropriate to geography and economics, or how the place is used, or how it makes people behave. Third, it may be understood as a changing reality, how it was, how it is, how it might be or why it differs. This last approach would suggest a historical or sociological study.

Each discipline offers a specialist approach, and can involve direct experience in observation, recording information and the presentation of findings, ideas and opinions. But a co-operative effort can provide a more coherent and meaningful experience for the pupil. Front Door suggests that an appropriate grouping to promote education in environmental design would be art, urban geography, social studies, history and English, and not the more accepted design department of art, craft and home economics. For, as Ken Baynes found in the study at the Royal College of Art, design education does not

*Above: fourth-year pupils at work.*

*Right: fifth-year work in ink and paper collage.*

depend on a particular school organisation, but is more influenced by the attitudes, aims and objectives of the teachers concerned. At Pimlico the school was organised on strict departmental lines, and co-operation between departments was not usual. At first contact with other departments was made informally, and ideas were exchanged on a basis of

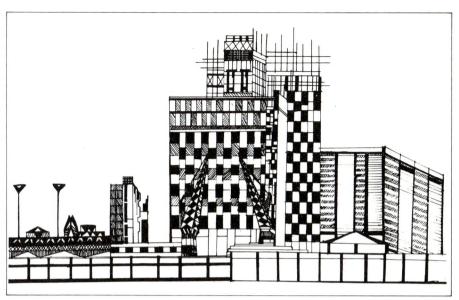

personal interest. After a number of exhibitions and seminars in the school, and attention from people outside the school, other departments began to realise the relevance of the Front Door work to the studies in which they were already involved, and made attempts to consider their work in relation to the possibilities offered by the Front Door courses.

One reaction was that departments had carefully considered and worked out their courses and did not feel able to become involved in more 'experimental work'. They perhaps felt rather insecure in a situation that did not depend on a 'body of knowledge' basis for course development, but preferred issue-based study and the development of attitudes and appreciation and criticism. This allowed an approach that fostered feeling and thoughts about things as being as important as one's knowlege about them. It seemed that because subject departments, working in isolation, were necessarily concerned with the development of their own courses, there was a danger either of neglect or duplication of work, or of work being done in one area less effectively than it could have been tackled elsewhere.

However, I do not think that inflexibility, either in departmental structure or the physical organisation of the school, is the main difficulty in coping with these large and important areas of educational experience; it is more to do with the inflexibility of teachers' attitudes. I think that education is necessarily about relationships; that we should consider what attitudes, concepts and skills we wish to develop in our pupils, and use this as our basis for communicating with each other, so that we capitalise on those things we have in common rather than exaggerate our differences as subject specialists.

'Apart from the concept of the academic syllabus, there is developing another and perhaps more fruitful approach; the development of environmental education as an education in awareness. Art education provides one important avenue. Since they are both the subject of visual appreciation, there is a natural link between art and the environment.'

*Offley Conference*

As an art teacher, I have been concerned with the development of visual and sensory awareness, and therefore involved with the usual range of activities in the art room. Then, through the experience of the Front Door project, I became increasingly aware of the need for art education to be seen in a much wider context than perhaps was normally the case.

I do not consider my job is primarily to teach children to paint or pot or print, but to promote the development of the child's perception and further his emotional and aesthetic development. I do not consider art as a frill, an extra, a recreational or a therapeutic activity, or as a subject more suitable for the 'practical' or less able child. Nor do I see it as a precious and specialist subject for the gifted few. I feel that the esoteric nature of art has very little relevance in the context of the school, but art itself should be a part of everyone's educational experience. We should, therefore, concentrate on the development of visual language as a means of understanding, expressing and communicating ideas. I believe that this should have a central place and that the development of visual literacy is as important as that of verbal literacy and numeracy. It is a relatively neglected part of the child's education, and I feel that art teachers should be prepared to be more assertive and outward looking.

I do see art as a specialist discipline with its own concepts and ways of understanding, but I also see it in the context of interdisciplinary study in relation to design or environmental education. Art teachers ought to be able to co-operate with any other subject discipline when it is necessary and advantageous to do so, because I can envisage links with just about every other subject department, or to be able to work on their own, doing their own thing, depending on the needs of the pupils and the types of work in which they are involved. This is why I am not happy about the faculty structure, as I feel it imposes a different type of strait-jacket from that imposed by rigid departmental boundaries. I therefore see the involvement of the art department as raising levels of response to environmental stimuli, and in interrelating visual study with other types of learning to enrich and enlarge other subject approaches to design and environmental education. The teacher should help the development of the child's visual language both in understanding and expression, and relate that language to his everyday world.

Thus there is no reason why visual education should happen only behind the door of the art studio. It should infiltrate other subject areas of the curriculum and spill out into the street. Bullock has advertised the need for teachers to consider the place of language across the curriculum. I think that teachers ought to consider the place of visual literacy in a wider context than they normally do. Thus art education based on environmental investigation provides rich educational opportunities for training in observation, the encouragement to think, research, compare, experiment, analyse and

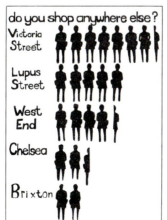

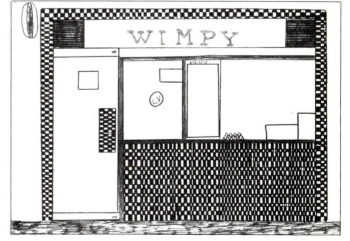

*Third-year: investigation and surveys.*

synthesise. Such experience leads to the development of positive attitudes and the ability to make qualitative judgements in relation to the environment . . . 'we see as much with our minds as with our eyes. We tend to see what we have learned to see, expect to see or want to see.'

According to Professor Bruce Archer, 'Design is that area of human experience, skill and knowledge that reflects man's concern with the appreciation and adaptation of his surroundings to the light of his material and emotional needs. In particular it relates to configuration, composition, meaning, value and purpose in man-made phenomena.'

I would suggest that design education has not adequately dealt with such a comprehensive field of study, but has tended to concentrate on graphic and product design, and has neglected environmental design. I can understand why. There is no one teacher in the school who is competent to deal with it. There is no teacher in the school who has been trained to deal

with it. I do not believe there is one subject in the school that can cope adequately with the complex and comprehensive nature of either design or environmental education, though there are many subjects that can involve themselves in both of these studies.

I believe that it is necessary and appropriate for teachers as educators to look at the curriculum and define their role and contribution in terms of both specialist and interdisciplinary study. As an art teacher I found myself attempting to teach art as well as educate through art, and in so doing contribute towards both environmental and design education. I think that every other subject teacher could reasonably view their role in similar terms.

I would therefore suggest that as teachers involved in design education we have a great responsibility for the development of attitudes towards the man-made environment, and that this aspect of the work is neglected at the expense of the promotion of craft skills. Peter Green suggests that:

*Above: fourth-year drawing – taxi rank.*

*Right: first-year drawing.*

'Materials for design education concentrate on skills and techniques without engaging teachers in the basic design issues. The tendency is still towards a rather superficial approach with the emphasis on style, skills and appearances. There is little thought provoking material about why things are designed and produced and whether they meet our needs.'

Just as in environmental or design education a number of teachers should pool their expertise and co-operate to discuss what they are doing, or could do in relation to other subjects, co-operating if necessary in the learning activity, we should also seek support from outside the school. The architects on the Front Door Project acted as an educational resource, environmental experts working with teachers as educational experts. I feel very strongly that teachers are not the only members of society with educational responsibilities, and I think that involving other people, whether 'experts' in a professional sense, or people with particular experience relevant to the study in hand, is a sensible approach that should be developed in other areas. This might be particularly relevant in home economics and craft departments. I do not suggest that we involve these outside experts so that children can copy professional practice, as I feel this has limited relevance in the classroom, but that we should invite such people to extend the learning possibilities, and provide an expertise to complement that of the teacher.

Local authorities have a statutory commitment to involve the public in planning decisions, but experience has indicated that there needs to be an increase in the provision made for environmental education to encourage more people to become involved in shaping their environment. Design or environmental education should therefore promote a greater preparedness to deal with design decisions in everyday life.

Three areas are identified where architects, or other outside experts, may be involved: in formulating projects, in the teaching situation, and in a supportive role as information source or adviser. In Front Door, the architects were used in all three areas, and were found to be of value in all of them. They were perhaps most useful in co-operating in the preparation of schemes and as a source of information, ideas and advice. Their involvement in the classroom was primarily to give them experience of the school situation, so that the planning of the work could be directly related to a particular age group and the limits imposed by the school organisation.

Another person who has educational responsibilities is the pupil himself, and I feel that generally pupils are not encouraged to be educationally responsible. They should be learning through their own direct experience of the world and be encouraged to take responsibility for their own education. Ken Baynes makes a pertinent remark in relation to this when he says:

'We give them a lot of practice in absorbing knowledge, little in reasoning or decision taking, hardly any in handling problems of appreciation.'

But much of design education provides a way in which learning is based on the child's experience – where he is encouraged to look, to understand, analyse, appreciate, make decisions, have opinions or express ideas. This I think is particularly true in relation to environmental investigation.

One aspect of this that became increasingly important in the Front Door project was that it was important to consider not only our own but the child's starting points. In many ways, the child's experience of the environment is very different from that of an adult. Of necessity, school courses are based on our own set of values as to what is important and significant. Perhaps it would be more constructive and creative if we were to try and base design and environmental education courses on the value system of the children we are teaching – that is to build on the perceptions and meanings with which the child invests his own environment.

This is what we attempted to do in the Front Door Project. The pupils, teachers and architects all found themselves in a learning situation, all had different types of experience and perceptions to bring to the work, and all were interdependent. The crux of the problem for the teacher was the creation of a learning environment in which a genuine and sincere response could be made.

*Eileen Adams was second in charge of the Art Department at Pimlico School, an 11 to 18 comprehensive, until the summer of 1976. She was the co-ordinator for the Front Door project for two years. At present she is seconded to the Schools Council Project 'Art and the Built Environment, 16 to 19' as the Project Officer. The aim of the study is to define the role of the Art Department in environmental education, and contact has been made with art teachers working in a variety of situations in a number of different environments.*

# Spondon School
## Wilf Ball and John Harahan

*Wilf Ball*

*John Harahan*

'*The design courses with which we are concerned at Spondon aim to encourage socially and environmentally aware students. Emphasis is placed, wherever possible, on the relationships between the students' understanding of their work and its context in our society, with practical work being centred in the local environment.*

'*We are concerned with developing students' attitudes to future change with a "living" content, as opposed to other subject areas, which often stress prescriptive knowledge boundaries.*

'*Parallels between the design process and the learning process have been made clear in recent years and are now central concepts in the emphasis on experience and the understanding of "products" within that context. In assessing the value of educational experience, this has led naturally to a particular interest in the importance of the students' records and communication of both experience and decisions made as a basis for accurate assessment of project work.*

'*It is impressive to observe the way in which students mature and become more rounded individuals through experiencing design courses. Much of the satisfaction in teaching derives from seeing this take place.*'

'It may be possible to specify that in the assessed work some practical skill must be presented and that practical work will play some part in the carrying through to the achievement of candidates' design work. The emphasis of assessment, however, may be expected to be placed on the intellectual, analytical and creating processes carried through in the preparation of a report.' (From the consultative document from the Schools Council commissioned feasibility study on Design in the proposed N and F-Level examinations.)

Design education takes many forms according to many factors, including the department or departments in which it is practised, and the training and experience of the teaching staff involved. One aspect, however, appears to be common to all forms and that is the importance accorded to the assessment of the *processes* of design activity as opposed to the *product*. This factor illustrates perhaps the main difference of emphasis between design education and the professional process of designing. Educationists are essentially concerned with discovering and giving credit for the quality of the education the young designer has experienced, while the professional designer is concerned almost entirely with the end product and its acceptability to his client.

It is impossible for the teacher to assess the extent and quality of experience unless the student records those experiences accurately and fully by one or more of the wide range of communication techniques available to him, both oral and visual. This must to some degree represent an account of the introspective relationship between the student and his work. Assessment is dependent on this to a major degree and therefore one could argue that such techniques are the most important skills that a design student learns.

This importance became critically evident to us with the first group of students who were submitted for the Oxford A83 Design examination. The comparative success of the major projects of two students was somewhat influenced by certain aspects of the recording of their two projects. Particularly significant were the omissions that affected the success of one of them. In the Chief Examiner's report for that year the two projects were briefly contrasted as examples:

'Comparing a model of a school building, which could be located anywhere, and a model of a proposed leisure centre to be located in a specified, real tract of English countryside.'

The examiner had quite rightly emphasised the importance of the student working to solve a real problem with real constraints against which his solutions could be measured, as opposed to an imaginary design situation in which the constraints could be manipulated by the student to suit himself. Genuine relevance is an important ingredient of all design experience, otherwise it is more than likely that a magic wand will secrete itself among the list of skills used by the young designer to solve his problems.

Returning to the two design problems in question, it is interesting to examine the circumstances that led to the situation which disturbed the assessor. In retrospect it can be seen that this was entirely due to the lack of communication of certain key information. The case studies that follow refer to the two projects concerned. They were both environmental, but quite different in content.

## The art/craft block

Stephen Oakes eventually decided on the brief: 'To design a comprehensive school art/craft block which would be suitable for use as an adult education centre.'

This brief grew out of a minor ergonomics project experienced in the lower-sixth year when Stephen investigated our existing upper-school art/craft block with special reference to lighting and noise problems associated with 'open-plan' workshop facilities. After composing a questionnaire, which was circulated to local art/craft departments, he produced drawings of an improved solution. Realising the faults of the existing block and that an ergonomic/architectural problem of this kind both interested him and also lent itself to the sort of major project that was eminently suited to his previous experience and skills, Stephen decided on his particular brief. In view of the increasing use of existing facilities by the local community, the latter part of the brief was an intelligent piece of social anticipation.

The major project started by making personal contact with Derby Architects and the Planning Department of the local Council, first for information in order to make a study of existing solutions in County schools (plans of new school facilities were made available by the authorities) and then for expert technical advice on the constraints discovered, including local building regulations, legal requirements on fire and safety, suppliers' and contractors' catalogues, and anything else that might have to be taken into account. This personal contact, especially with the Architects' Department, continued throughout the project and was very rewarding as it gave Stephen an insight into professional practice. Indeed, it made available to him the expertise that enabled him to present his final report in a most professional form, showing an eye for detail as well as skill in draughtsmanship. After a most industrious investigation and assessment of needs and possibilities the final solution was reached. Individually designed spaces were provided for:

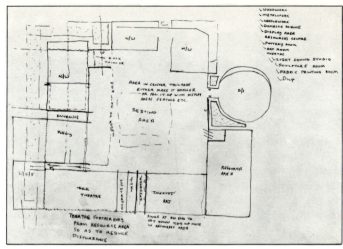

| | |
|---|---|
| Woodwork | Resources Centre |
| Metalwork | Display Areas |
| Technical Drawing | Locker Areas |
| Needlework | Office and Reprographic |
| Domestic Science | Theatre |
| Art | Medical Rooms |
| Pottery | Rest Room |
| Sculpture | Coffee Bar |
| Fabric | Staff Rooms |
| Light/Sound Studio | Store Rooms |
| Dark Rooms | Toilets |

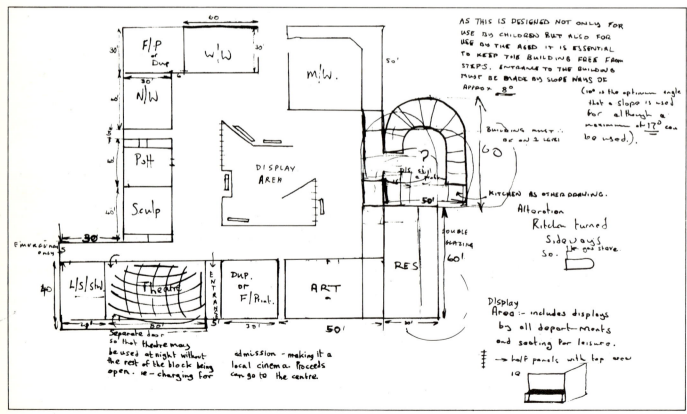

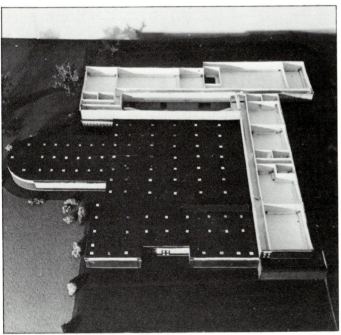

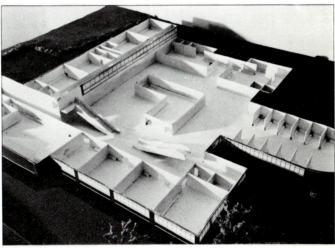

*Opposite: rough sketches of two alternative layouts for the building.*

*Left: the completed model.*

*Below left and below: the model with the roof partly removed and completely removed.*

Rough sketches of alternative solutions for relative shapes and positions of these spaces were used to facilitate a final choice of optimum solutions. The position of equipment, fittings and internal surfaces was decided in the same way.

A three-dimensional scale model in reinforced card was then produced on a base landscaped with grp, and the interior was painted white to give the greatest possible clarity to the relative form and size of spaces. The exterior imitated closely the various textures and colours of cladding units available from sources used by the Local Authority. The final result might be considered to be a detailed, carefully researched, but conventional architectural solution.

The short time available for evaluation meant that only the comments of the Architects' Department were sought. However, Stephen showed critical awareness in his own evaluation of the success of his solutions and made a technical evaluation of the construction of the final model, including tests such as the relative amount of warping produced by different surface treatments – sealers, slow and quick drying paints etc. An idea of the detail of his evaluation can be gained from the following excerpts from his documentation:

'I am pleased with the basic design of the building – there are only two rooms that have not turned out as well as they should. They are the woodwork and the metalwork rooms, and they will probably not get enough light from outside. This might have been improved somewhat by the addition of two sets of

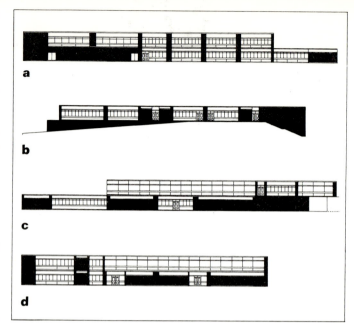

*Right: exterior elevations of the building.*

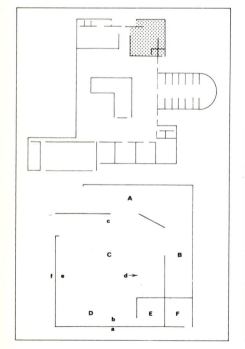

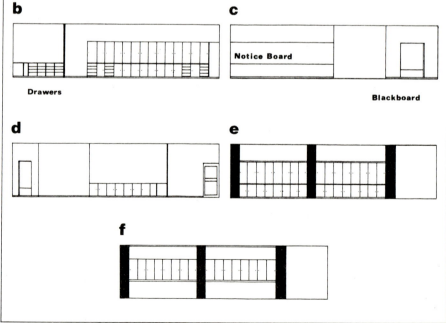

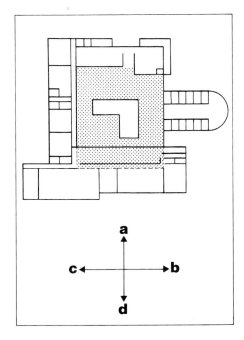

*Above: plan of lower floor, display area shaded.*

*Above right: details of interior walls of display area.*

*Opposite far left: general plan of lower floor, metalwork room shaded.*
*Details of metalwork room:*
*A Metal store*
*B Cutting room*
*C General work area*
*D Machine area*
*E Finished work store*
*F Gas bottle store*

*Opposite left: details of interior walls of metalwork room.*

skylights – these are not shown on the final drawings, but are shown on the model.

'The fabric printing, needlework, pottery, sculpture and art rooms are on the first floor and therefore get natural light from two directions. This is one point that was considered from the start. There is access to the first floor either by steps or a ramp. This is a good point in that young mothers with prams etc and elderly people will be able to gain access to any part of the building. The practical block is to cater for approximately 330 students, and I therefore think that there are not enough lavatories for the number of people. More lavatories could be provided underneath the pottery and sculpture room where at the moment there is only earth. The staff rooms could have been connected by a spiral staircase so as to make them into a more united area. This staircase would also have served as another way from first to ground floor in emergency, although there are enough exit routes already.

'I am pleased with the theatre as it can be isolated from the rest of the building and used for public performances without disturbing evening classes at work. The colour of the exterior panels could have been a bit lighter, but I am very pleased with the blue brick colour.'

## Outdoor pursuits centre

'To design an outdoor pursuits centre for the Manifold Valley, Derbyshire.'

This was the brief that Kim Foo set himself as his major project. This project arose from Kim's keen interest in open-air activities, and particularly his knowledge of the area concerned which, although popular with the public, had no organised facilities. A photographic survey of significant parts of the valley was initially made to illustrate possible sites for various proposed units.

After a comprehensive study of alternative sites along the valley, the optimum position of the proposed centre and other facilities was decided upon. Maps and sketches illustrated these alternatives and final decisions. These dealt particularly carefully with access, detailed facilities and investigations into technical requirements, none of which sticks in the mind more than a carefully researched study concerning the type of generator needed to provide power for the Centre, which would be in an area lacking all services.

In order to provide facilities for canoeing, the river being too shallow, a dam was designed and sited, as well as an ingenious canoeing instruction facility at the centre itself. The dam was to be built across the River Hamps near the centre, rather than across the Manifold, which is above an underground cavern into which the water drains through limestone faults. Kim was well aware of this interesting local tourist attraction, where in summer the river disappears, to reappear some distance away. Most other recognised outdoor pursuits already take place in the area, but lack adequate amenities.

The Centre itself was then designed, based upon the types of activity anticipated and numbers involved (statistics of local visitors were used for this). Kim paid particular attention to keeping the building in harmony with the environment. Exterior cladding was to be in natural materials, usually wood, and camping and parking sites were placed in unobtrusive spots. There were several ingenious and novel ideas in some of the facilities. For example, it was proposed to place felled trees and tree stumps at strategic points in the camp site. Built into these were to be power points into which campers could plug minor appliances. Litter bins were to be hollow logs placed vertically and seats were to be formed from logs.

A great deal of time was spent on finding a realistic solution to problems of water supply and drainage. The first was found

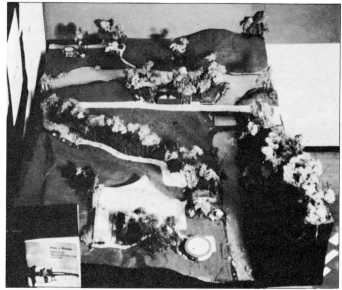

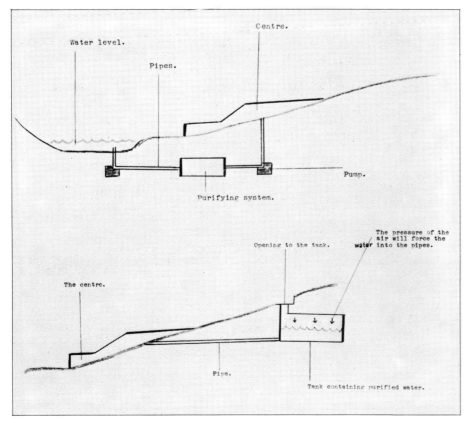

Water level.

Pipes.

Centre.

Pump.

Purifying system.

The pressure of the air will force the water into the pipes.

Opening to the tank.

The centre.

Pipe.

Tank containing purified water.

*Ideas for solving the problems of water supply.*

*'While visiting Beeston Tor I went and talked to the farmer who worked the surrounding land. He told me that water was piped to his home from a nearby reservoir. This means that the Centre could also have water piped from the reservoir, or run off the farmer's pipes.'*

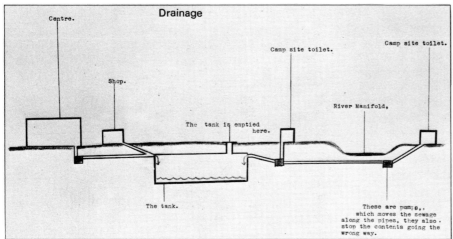

## Drainage

Centre.

Shop.

Camp site toilet.

Camp site toilet.

River Manifold,

The tank is emptied here.

The tank.

These are pumps, which moves the sewage along the pipes, they also stop the contents going the wrong way.

*Details of site drainage.*

*'Drainage can be difficult and expensive. In very hard land there have to be close drains and the soil must be improved, but this is costly. A gentle slope helps surface water to run off. It may also reduce the cost of any drainage scheme that may be needed, and allows drains to be discharged into open ditches, streams, storm-water drains, pumping schemes or soak-aways.'*

to be comparatively simple as local farmers had piped water laid on and it would be no problem to use this facility. Drainage problems involved investigations into types of drains and their relative costs, using Building Bulletin 28 – *Drainage of rain water and drainage from buildings*.

Realising that the Centre would undoubtedly be used a good deal by schools, facilities for educational parties were designed. Apart from domestic facilities for housing and feeding up to 50 pupils, other educational facilities were planned. In addition to a nature trail being devised, a circular building was designed as a museum. The area is of considerable archaeological interest as important prehistoric remains have been found in Thor's Cave and in a pothole at Beeston Tor. A classroom and resources area completed the educational facilities. Eventually the Centre was designed to include:

Workshop, canoe and potholing store room

Dormitories

Staff accommodation and office

Medical room

Climbing room

Kitchen

Dining room

Showers

Common room

Classroom

Resources area

Boys' toilet

Girls' toilet

Other facilities outside the main building included:

Stables with living quarters above

Museum

Water services

Power services

Drainage

Camping site

Warden's bungalow

The river dam

Improved roads

Diesel storage building

Housing for two generators (one small one for emergencies)

# Nature Trail

1   The trail starts at the museum
2   Along the river bank people on the trail can notice how the river has worn away the banks
3   Stepping stones
4   Along the road and the river bank people can observe the vegetation and any animals
5   Bridge. This bridge is made out of natural stone. It was made by farmers for the river is too deep for them to take their livestock across
6   In summer the river disappears into an underground cavern, this can be seen here
7   While walking up the hill there are large round pits in the ground which can be seen. From these animals receive their food in winter
8   Top of the hill – from here the whole area can be observed
9   Descending the hill. The vegetation can be noticed once again. The trees are at an angle for the wind has caused them to bend
10  Ski slopes
11  The Centre
12  The shop. Also the canoeing area can be seen
13  A disused railway bridge takes you across the river
14  The trail now takes you through a wood
15  A typical farm. The teacher might be able to gain permission from the farmer to look around his farm
16  Stepping stones
17  Pothole. Primitive man used to live inside. If the teacher wishes he can ask someone at the Centre to show them inside the pothole, otherwise it can be dangerous to go inside without someone who is experienced
18  Beeston Tor – notice the rock formations
19  If you wish you can go to the top of Beeston Tor
20  Descend back to the museum

**Table 1**

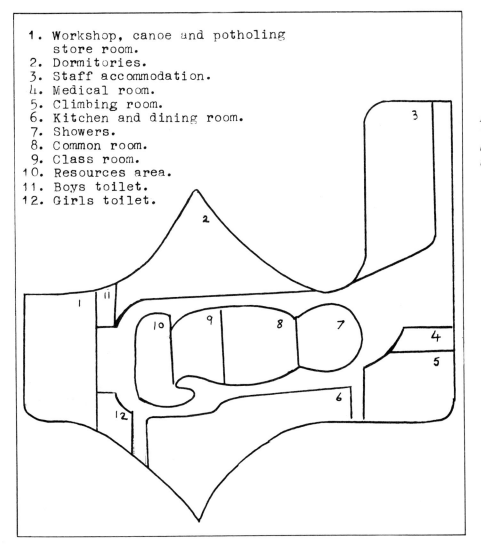

1. Workshop, canoe and potholing store room.
2. Dormitories.
3. Staff accommodation.
4. Medical room.
5. Climbing room.
6. Kitchen and dining room.
7. Showers.
8. Common room.
9. Class room.
10. Resources area.
11. Boys toilet.
12. Girls toilet.

*Plan of the Centre.*
*'I am satisfied with the shape of the Centre, but I feel there is not enough room within it to house 50 pupils and 16 teachers.'*

The outstanding characteristic of the drawings of the centre was the way they reflected Kim's natural interest in sculptural form – all spaces were free forms rather than geometrical ones, even the shape of the large dining table was strikingly sculptural. Naturally this created a conflict between aesthetic appearance and normal building practice. Standard fittings might have had to be adjusted, especially in view of the rarity of right angles in the design. However, the spaces were stimulating and in keeping with external natural forms in a way that much modern individual domestic architectural design has developed. Novelty of concepts in designing is rare among designers of any age and is to be nourished if originality is not to be overwhelmed by the mass of conventional solutions. In this case it made the whole design into a very personal statement by a student particularly sensitive to spatial form and relationships. The plan of the Centre itself illustrates this.

Kim then constructed a large three-dimensional landscape model using papier-mâché, cast resin for water, card for buildings and natural objects such as twigs for trees. This use of natural materials produced a most effective open-air look for the model. This is apparent where the figure using the stepping stones to cross the river looks quite real, so full of the atmosphere of the outdoors is the model. Admittedly the use of out-of-focus foliage by the student photographer has added to this effect. These are the extra dimensions one might expect from a design student with a leaning towards aesthetics. A technical student might have concentrated entirely on the buildings and facilites and thus omitted a significant dimension in the model's efficiency of communication.

Kim evaluated his solutions by comparison with his original criteria, giving a list of items where he felt his solution could be considered deficient in some aspect. He also made a critical appraisal of the actual model – the materials and techniques used and its aesthetic quality.

Kim was generally satisfied with the facilities designed, but to his chagrin had found that the site for his dam was still above porous strata and that gradual seepage would make it impossible to maintain water for canoeing.

It was noticeable that he was more concerned in his evaluation about aesthetic qualities in his solutions than Stephen. This compensated for the fact that he recognised that the conflict between original forms and modern technological

# Advantages

The Centre and the other buildings in the surrounding area blend in with the environment.

The Centre can organise a variety of activities within the area because the facilities are available.

The drainage water and electrical systems should prove to be adequate and efficient.

# Disadvantages

To produce a centre of this type would be very expensive. (This is because a great deal of earth would have to be moved.)

Since the buildings are built upon the river's banks, if flooding arises the buildings would stop functioning.

The water will escape from the dammed river because the rock underneath the river used is very porous.

Water running down the hill-side will collect on the flat land causing it to become marshy.

tendencies towards standardised units in building made it very unlikely that his design of the spaces in the centre could be a practical possibility. On the other hand, the solutions of Stephen's work were decided on realistic constraints against a background of legal requirements and existing building practice. There is no doubt that this solution forms a genuine, even if conventional, possibility.

The examiner's remarks emphasise the importance of the student selecting a real problem of need in a specific situation. Working to real constraints against which solutions can be tested is a much more significant experience than dealing with hypothetical problems in imaginary situations. Kim's work clearly satisfies this requirement and presumably his marks for this project benefited. Stephen's work, however, would obviously be assessed according to the very general brief he had chosen. The importance of full documentation and especially a clear and specific brief are highlighted here. As relevant information was not included in Stephen's major project documentation, the Examiner was unaware of the connection between this project and the support project by which he had

been previously stimulated. Moreover, the brief should have specified that the architectural complex was intended to replace the existing school art/craft block on the same site. As it did not, many areas of relevance were not available to the Examiner. An element of failure in communication thus affected this student's success to a significant extent.

These two case studies also highlight another problem of assessment. Where design problems in very different areas are studied – fine art on the one hand, scientific or technical on the other, for example – how is it possible to compare the two solutions with any accuracy? Although many criteria can be seen to be common to both, some will be more relevant to one than the other. Can any form of assessment be fair to both? We feel that it can.

The teacher should have been closely involved with all stages of the student's work and so long as teacher assessment is used as well as expert external moderation, there should be little difficulty. During the years we have been involved in the assessment of our own students' practical projects in the Oxford A83 Design examination, we have found its assessment form very effective in this respect. As our students choose their problem area according to their own aptitudes and interests, we have had widely differing projects tackled and assessed with commendable perception and accuracy. The assessment forms for A83 major projects are shown at the end of this chapter, and it will be seen that due credit is given to both intuitive and rational aspects of designing. The problem in these two case studies was not one of subject area, but one of communication by the students of all the information necessary for accurate assessment.

*Wilf Ball is the Head of the Faculty of Creative Studies at Spondon School, Derby, an 11 to 18 comprehensive with over 1900 pupils. In the first three years the students rotate on a foundation course investigating materials, tools and techniques, and after the third year the school offers a wide range of examination courses. Several project based CSE Mode III courses are offered as well as the traditional O- and A-level and CSE syllabuses. A Mode III Design course and O-level Design course have in recent years begun feeding interested students into the Oxford A-level Design course.*

*He was a member of the Schools Council Steering Committee set up to produce an N and F Design syllabus involving project work in any area of the curriculum. He was for a time editor for the Council of the National Association for Design Education.*

| **A83 DESIGN**<br>(Assessment form A) | **PROJECT ASSESSMENT**<br>Project Title: | | |
|---|---|---|---|
| **Heading** | **RATING**  Tick one box per row | | |
| Comprehension of project as a whole? | No significant omissions | Project considered in very wide context | Adequate scope of relevant factors |
| Identification of need for information? | All necessary areas recognised | Most facets of project were considered | Showed adequate foresight |
| Thoroughness in gaining information: by experiment etc. | Experiments thoroughly exploited | Experiments etc. competently performed | Experiments performed adequately |
| Ditto: by search and consultation? | Widest possible range of sources explored | Several types of source extensively searched | Reasonable coverage achieved |
| Decisions intelligently based on available evidence? | Available evidence carefully weighed | Considerable logical deduction was used | Reasonable amount of thought given |
| Consideration of several possible solutions? | Range of possibilities identified and explored | Several other possibilities properly considered | At least one alternative considered |
| Planning and organisation of work | Tight control on current target | Intelligent changes of target as circumstances changed | Reasonable ability to manage time and effort |
| How well was project chosen (considering resources and need)? | Saw real need which could be achieved | Sound target based on slight deficiency in recognising resources or vice versa | Reasonable need based on adequate recognition of resources |
| Quality of manufacture and assembly – having regard to demands of project? | Own limitations and demands of design well recognised | Good overall, but with slight deficiencies | Adequate degree of skill achieved |
| Completeness of report? | Very complete and detailed record | All aspects covered, but in variable depth | Rather patchy |
| How well does report justify project and evaluation? | Covers underlying thinking completely | Very revealing about underlying thinking | Good in some areas |
| How well is the report itself designed? | Well organised and most competently made | Shows attention to detail, and thought in its layout | Adequate, but not striking in any respect |
| How well and aptly has the candidate illustrated ideas? | Well-chosen, varied illustration; fair level of skill | Fair level of skill, some reservation on variety or aptness | Adequately chosen and reasonably executed |
| How well was project evaluated (on own actions)? | Comprehensive review of own actions | Very fair review of own actions | Reasonable or adequate second view of *some* actions |
| How well was project evaluated (with reference to design process)? | Able to give good criticism dispassionately | A good criticism with a few 'blind-spots' | Recognises some significant reasons for redesign |
| Natural flair for, and sensitivity to, design? | A natural, fluent and sensitive designer | Markedly good in this respect | Average in this respect |
| Where would you place this project? | Top 10% | Top 25% | In the middle |

| SCHOOL | | CANDIDATE | TUTOR | |
|---|---|---|---|---|
| | | **Teacher Involvement** | | **JUSTIFICATION** |
| | | Which heading needed *most* help? | Which heading needed *least* help? | Where appropriate refer to the report; the 'product'; log book; notes, or sketches; tutor's impression; any other factors. |
| Few additional factors outside immediate target | Very limited view indeed | | | |
| Only limited need for information recognised | Saw no need for any information | | | |
| Only rather trivial tests performed | No tests worthy of the name | | | |
| *Some* information was acquired | No real sources consulted | | | |
| Some thought was given to evidence | Decisions taken on random basis | | | |
| Existence of other possibilities recognised | No other possibilities considered | | | |
| Recognised some need for planning | Worked in a very haphazard fashion | | | |
| Failed to discern need properly, or resources dimly recognised | Unsound choice, no recognition of resources etc. | | | |
| Shows some evidence of skill in limited area | Cannot recognise own limits or demands of project | | | |
| Significant areas omitted | Only a very shallow description | | | |
| Gives a very limited picture of the context of project | Gives little or no justification | | | |
| Little more than a diary | Shoddy and ill-organised | | | |
| Leaves something to be desired all round | Little recognition of role of illustration | | | |
| Only limited ability to review own progress | Unable to see actions in any other light | | | |
| Only limited ability to review own design | Unable to criticise own design | | | |
| Shows only limited ability | Unfortunately no real innate design ability | | | |
| Lower 25% | Bottom 10% | | | |

**A83 DESIGN**
(Assessment form B)

**GENERAL ASSESSMENT OF PRACTICAL WORK**

**Heading 1**

**Rating 2** (tick one box below)

| | The only real reservation is that noted in column 3 | Some reservations but quality is still adequate | There are several good points but aspects could be covered much better |
|---|---|---|---|
| **Dissertation** Relevance of practical work | | | |
| Quality of argument | | | |
| Recognition of design approach | | | |
| **Properties of materials** Comparative knowledge of materials | | | |
| Comparative knowledge of processes | | | |
| **Criticism of products** Range and relevance of criteria | | | |
| Recognition of production and user aspects | | | |
| Ability to compare products of varying types | | | |
| **Preliminary design work** Ability to consider level of requirement | | | |
| Ability to consider several possible answers | | | |
| Quality of chosen design | | | |
| **Skills** – *intelligent exploration* with regard to candidate's previous experience | Complete for at least *two* materials | | |
| **Ergonomic  Psychological  Economic** How far has candidate recognised, the various influences and their effects? | Only *one* of the three areas is required | | |

| SCHOOL | | CANDIDATE | TUTOR |
|---|---|---|---|
| | | **Justification 3**<br>Enter the feature on which column 2 is completed<br><br>Give feature, the inclusion of which gives a high rating, or the omission of which leads to a lower rating. If necessary, indicate the appropriate work listed in column 4 | **List of exercises and other work done 4** |
| The only *good* point is that entered in column 3<br>Candidate is deficient | No score | | |
| | | | |
| | | | |
| | | | |
| | | | |
| | | | |
| | | | |
| | | | |
| | | | |
| | | | |
| | | | |

# Acknowledgements

Many people have given a great deal of help in compiling this book for which I wish to express my thanks and gratitude.

First, the contributors themselves, who have provided the substance around which the book is compiled, have made the editing an interesting task and patiently accepted comments and suggested changes. The students whose activities have been described also truly deserve thanks for allowing their particular enthusiams to be recorded.

My experience at the Department of Design Research, Royal College of Art, working on the 'Design in General Education' project, was for me important and formative. I would like to thank Richard Langdon and Ken Baynes whose professional approach and good humour were inspiring, and the team members and friends who made my work there so enjoyable.

I must also thank Phil Roberts, whose perceptive criticisms have considerably affected my attitudes and ideas; Don Fairhall at Bishop Lonsdale College, who gave me initial direction; and Wilf Ball, a colleague and friend whose unfailing optimism is continually encouraging and who introduced me to design education as a student teacher.

My wife, Linda, has undertaken a great deal of work in helping with this book. Not only has she patiently typed the numerous letters and various typescripts involved, but also managed to produce a son at the same time.

I am grateful to the following: the GLC Architects' Department and the Department of the Environment for permission to use the photographs from the Front Door project; Omer Roucoux for the photographs from Manshead School; Malcolm Deere, the Chief Examiner of the Oxford A-level for permission to reproduce the assessment forms, and the team at the Design Council who asked me to undertake this work and made the whole project possible.